BANTU CONTRIBUTION IN BRAZILIAN POPULAR MUSIC: ETHNOMUSICOLOGICAL PERSPECTIVES

BANTU CONTRIBUTION IN BRAZILIAN POPULAR MUSIC: ETHNOMUSICOLOGICAL PERSPECTIVES

KAZADI WA MUKUNA

Translated from the Portuguese by Diasporic Africa Press

DIASPORIC AFRICA PRESS

This book is a publication of

DIASPORIC AFRICA PRESS
NEW YORK | WWW.DAFRICAPRESS.COM

Copyright © 2014 Diasporic Africa Press, Inc.

All rights reserved. No part of this publication may be reproduced or distributed in any form or by any means, or stored in a database or retrieval system, without the prior written permission of the publisher.

ISBN-13: 978-1-937306-25-0
Library of Congress Control Number: 2014938288

Author's note: the author would like to thank family, friends, colleagues, and students of his, including Deanna Nebel, who helped with a number of the musical transcriptions in this book.

CONTENTS

Preface	*i*
Foreword	*v*
Introduction	*ix*
Part I: *Redefinition*	*xv*
Chapter 1 A Redefinition of the Enslaved Bantu Peoples	*1*
Part II *Identification and Determination*	*35*
Chapter 2 Identification of Bantu Musical Elements	*37*
Chapter 3 Determination of Cultural Origins of Identified Bantu Musical Elements	*65*
Part III *Mutation, Persistence, and Continuity*	*95*
Chapter 4 Conceptual Mutation and Bantu Musical Elements in the Popular Traditions of Brazil	*97*
Chapter 5 Persistence and Continuity of Bantu Musical Elements in Brazil	*127*
Conclusion	*139*
Bibliography	*141*
Notes	*159*
Index	*171*

PREFACE

I will never forget the day and the circumstances in which I met my good friend Kazadi. Recalling this event, we will set the time machine to the geographic point of 24°S, 47°W, with an estimated date of November 2, 1975.

Making some adjustments, I can see a classroom full of students where I am giving a lecture in English on an esoteric topic: "Characteristic Traces of Angola in African-Brazilian Music." This was the first of ten lectures in a course on Bantu expansions and its presence in Brazil, which I delivered at the Center for African Studies at the University of São Paulo that year.

Our unusual encounter happened thanks to an invitation from the director of the center, Professor Fernando A. A. Mourão, who had been uncomfortable with researchers' strong emphasis on a particular element (Nago/Gege) from the Guinea Coast in the African-Brazilian cultural panorama. In his trips to Angola, Mourão realized that the Bantu language speakers—in south-central Angola and even in southeast of Africa—had indeed contributed to the cultural texture of Brazilian and other related cultural groups. Thus, he invited researchers and students from Central Africa to give lectures. One of these postgraduate students was Kazadi wa Mukuna from the Democratic Republic of the Congo, then Zaire. In 1975, Kazadi had completed his graduate studies in ethnomusicology at the University of California, Los Angeles, and was then studying at University of São Paulo for a second doctorate in sociology.

Well, there he was, sitting in my audience, ignorant of our heavenly kinship. He wondered what the *mundele* (white man) would say and how much he really knew about Central Africa. At that time, my lecture on the Angolan peculiarities in Brazilian music had already become routine. Actually, I was preparing a book on this subject using the material from my research in Angola, and had been testing the reaction of Brazilian audiences throughout the previous year during a trip to Salvador/Bahia and other places where I went with Donald Kachamba to give lectures.

In 1975, however, I was alone in Brazil. I started to play some Angolan songs to the audience in that classroom, including *likembe* (*mbira*) *lamellophone*. These songs, which I had learned in 1965, were by Kufuna Kandonga in Angola (who later died in the Angolan civil war). When I started playing, I knew something was missing—the sticks—to play the famous asymmetrical passage of sixteen pulses called *kachacha* in eastern Angola. My eyes searched the audience for help. They fell on Kazadi, who was sitting quietly, and I felt that I needed to approach him. I put the two sticks in his hands and asked him to play the pattern while I played *likembe*.

Of course, the *likembe* was quite familiar to him. It had been the instrument for personal entertainment in Central Africa during the first half of the twentieth century, before gradually being replaced by the electric guitar. Kazadi was already a great connoisseur of the electric guitar history and traditions emerging in Congo/Zaire from 1940 to 1970, and had examined almost all the published records during his stay at UCLA, including those of the famous Ngoma produced by Firm Jeronimidis in Kinshasa (Léopoldiville).[1] So during the 1950s, *likembe* was part of a musical pre-show in Kinshasa.

Kazadi took my sticks and together we played. Actually, he thought I wanted him to play another configuration with my songs, but our communication and our understanding were immediate. I don't think the audience noticed how quickly we adapted to each other. When I realized that he was ready to play another sequence, I interrupted and simply told him: "No, you play *ngbo ngbo ngbo ngbolo ngbo ngbolo!*" Thus, he played it. These were the roots of our friendship: immediate communication and understanding.

We met two years later in Kinshasa. At that time, Donald Kachamba was with me and I was able to see the pleasure on Kazadi's face when Donald (on electric guitar) and I (on clarinet) were playing our own composition, "Lubumbashi Liumba." That was unforgettable....

There was a special event in 1979. It was in that year the Portuguese edition of of Kazadi's *Contribuição Bantu na Música Popular Brasileira*) appeared for the first time. The coincidence was that both of us had written our books on related subjects, which were published in the same year; his about general Bantu contributions and mine about Angolan peculiarities. This was not the only reason to celebrate, but there was a deeper meaning in the religious concepts of *umbanda*.[2]

The profound meaning was that our terrestrial itineraries had converted into two compass points of transcendence expressed by the combinations of numbers 7 and 5, and 7 and 9. Seven plus five is the structure of the passage of pulse 12 and seven plus nine is the structure of the passage of pulse 16, both numbers defining the two compass points of the asymmetrical universe. In 1975, we met for the first time, and in 1979 we had published together. Kazadi's book was his doctoral thesis at the Center for African Studies at the University of São Paulo, and has been influential since then.

Of course, this was not his first book. Before I met Kazadi for the first time in 1975, he had already published a volume on nursery rhymes called *The Characteristics of the Vocal Music of the Luba-Shankadi Children* and articles resulting from his studies of the history of urban Congolese music had become very well known in scholarly circles. Luba denoted a linguistic-cultural group of southern DRC, where he was born.

Throughout the years, I have visited Kazadi many times in Kent, Ohio. Here, he is currently spending one of the most productive periods of his career—publishing lots of articles about the history and the formation of urban music styles in Congo/Zaire, African-Brazilian traditions such as the folkloric drama *Bumba-meu-boi*, and so on. He has completed a new book based on his extensive research in Maranhão, Brazil—*The Ox and the Slave: A Satirical Musical Folk Drama in Maranhão*.

Fortunately, the present book has been translated from Brazilian Portuguese to English. As an essential work on the African-Brazilian ethnomusicology, this book offers access to almost everything that has been and is being written about African-Brazilian music. Unfortunately, this work was unavailable for many years despite the constant demand from academic circles.

Not only is Kazadi's writing in demand, but so is his CD *Mchanganyiko wa Muziki wa ki Afrika* (*Medley of African Music*) performed with a musical group including Kazadi and his students from Kent State University. I had the divine opportunity to see the group present its music in an event organized by the Department of Pan-African Studies, to celebrate the fortieth anniversary of *Things Fall Apart* from Chinua Achebe.

Gerhard Kubik

FOREWORD

The systematic study of the African presence in Brazil starts with the use of a dichotomous concept in the published works that specifically address African origins. It divides the African contribution into the coming of the Bantu people and the Sudanese people. It established a system that was transmitted by subsequent works and focused on the cultural aspects of this contribution. It did not take into account, however, the fact that the distinction between the Bantu and the Sudanese is essentially a linguistic one. The Sudanese contribution is rewarded systematically and the Bantu contribution is not taken into account for lack of a culture.

The main problem is a lack of specificity in African culture in general. The transatlantic analogy is hampered by the lack of better scientific information. Only recently, studies have started to underline the fundamental concepts of African thought, which, until now, was an unknown or partially treated subject. Isolated and seemingly exotic aspects present themselves as a constant part of a cultural nature. These aspects are primarily a result of the colonial process in its basic phase: The transatlantic trade centered on enslaved Africans from the fifteenth century to the nineteenth century, and was a response to the needs of the industrial revolution.

Thus ideas about African religious practices spread based on facts that are a result of a long process of anomie. Among them is the concept of a "wizard," a facet of the traditional healer, whose practices are a response to the situation of both structural and psychological social disintegration. An autonomous concept of religion emerges when, in a communal tradition, it is found in every moment of daily life.

The dissemination of African thought is a very recent phenomenon. In the scientific field, it is a subject limited to a few experts who know the persistent concepts disseminated from a comparative vision and evolutionary nature that justified, in ethical terms, the dependent situation of the African continent. In this perspective, the problem is posed in terms of comparison with the colonizer culture, which always favored the latter. From a series of partial studies, one can arrive at a concept about an African cultural unit.

Studies carried out in the Sudanese sphere, different from the Bantu sphere, demonstrate and validate the principle of an African cultural unity in terms of the principles or fundamental concepts of the world as conceived by the Africans, as well as minor specific differences within these spheres. In this line of thought, we reference the works of Cheihk Anta Diop, Marcel Griaule, R. P. Placide Tempels, Louis-Vicent Thomas, René Lineau, Alexis Kagame, and many other authors. The differences, primarily at the formal level, are hypothetical. They should be the vicissitudes of an evolving historical process, and are expressed by a moral density, according to the concept of structural functionalism based on Emil Durkheim's idea of social solidarity regarding divisions of labor.[3]

The works related to an African cultural presence in Brazil or even in the Americas are extremely general, or they depart from secondhand knowledge obtained from the African continent that is later compared with the Americas or other specific regions. Some authors such as Melville J. Herskovits, however, researched specific areas from both sides of the Atlantic. Among the Brazilian authors, Arthur Ramos started to design an extended research trip to the African continent with the goal of reevaluating his works based on his new perspectives on African culture. Unfortunately, his premature death did not allow him to carry out his plan. Among authors who specifically analyze African origins, we find Pierre Verger, who performed a series of studies in Brazil, Nigeria, and Benin, which have made important contributions. Among other authors, I would name Tiago de Oliveira Pinto, who has contributed valuably to studies of Candomble, *capoeira*, and *samba*; Kabengele Munanga and his studies of racial relations in Brazil; Mariano Carneiro da Cunha, also conducting research in Brazilian and Nigerian spaces simultaneously; Carlos Henriques Serrano in Angola; Henrique de Oliveira in Algeria; and Fabio da Rocha Leite on the Ivory Coast. In Salvador, Vivaldo Costa Lima and Yeda de Castro, after an internship in Nigeria and later in the Democratic Republic of the Congo (DRC), conducted a comparative study between the Yorùbá and Bantu languages in terms of their presence and influence in the Bahia state. Among the foreign authors, I would name Professor Gerhard Kubik at the University of Vienna, in the specific field of musicology; and American professors such as Gérard Behague, in the field of popular and erudite music, and Jerry Michael Turner who researched aspects of the slave trade between Dahomey and Brazil. The results of these and future studies will permit us to examine the African cultural presence in relation to Brazilian culture in a more systematic way and from concrete data, a result of research in both areas.

The author of *Bantu Contribution in Brazilian Popular Music* did not intend to solve an academic dispute. But without a doubt, his work enlists those works which constitute an objective contribution to the study of the African presence in Brazilian culture, and provides an element of greater validity for the future discussion of this academic controversy. The analysis was carried out on the evolution of Bantu music in Africa, which was a result of colonization and cultural addition to its African origins. This analysis has allowed for a better conceptualization of the problem, without creating dangerous generalizations.

The author used empirical data collected during his research and the historical and sociological literature, and then carried out an analysis that emphasized the process that has led to changes and explains the act of artistic creation. Kazadi wa Mukuna makes another central point. While many authors present aspects of African culture, such as music, strictly linked to a functional scheme, Kazadi emphasizes that "in Brazil, it is realized...such as the example of what occurred with the creation of the modern music of the DRC during the colonial period (emergence of worker camps around the headquarters of the companies of economic exploitation), that there is the persistence in the organological structure of musical instruments, the cycle of the rhythmic patterns and the sacrifice of their cultural values."

From an aesthetic point of view, the author provides rich evidence from the Bantu form of music. Studying individuals and specific productions, he shows the universality of the aesthetic perspective by analyzing the major lines of the content and form. The music and the rhythms are forces of a global system of thought and action, but escaped from their cultural content to address.

One of Kazadi wa Mukuna's merits is that his work is not closed or finished, but extremely open. In his work, the empirical materials are subjected to theoretical treatment, without which it imposes itself, creates new dogmas, reinforces certain claims, or inserts itself before the author works in the field of a dynamic production. It analyzes and compares situations in terms of space and time by combining two methodologies—one musical and other sociological—without dichotomizing society and music. It uses empirical data, either in relation to the music itself or to the musical instruments.

Kazadi wa Mukuna has commendedly solved the problem related to the transmission of the Bantu musical elements from generation to generation. He resorted to Maurice Halbwach's concept of memory, and, on a theoretical plane, he knew how to transition from social psychology to society, resorting to the works of Georges Balandier and Roger Bastide. He used and analyzed, through his own research material, the concept of mutation. The sociological analysis did not harm the treatment of musicology. The analysis of this point of view followed a specific and autonomous methodology, and served the empirical material well in terms of sociological explanation. The author addresses African musical structures—their persistence and the mutations in the Brazilian and African spaces—from musicological and sociological perspectives, offering us a balanced and thus original study that will certainly uncover new clues in the research on Brazilian music, a subject that lately has been gaining the attention of scholars in various fields. As the author rightly says, "The conceptual mutation was an adaptation of musical elements in the style of the new society," and we believe that, in many cases, the musical elements are linked "to the *muntu* identity" by their rhythm.

Fernando Augusto de Albuquerque Mourão

INTRODUCTION

The origin and date of introduction of the *samba* in Brazilian popular music have been controversial among scholars. Over the past decades, several authors have discussed the origin of the word *samba*, which is associated with a form of music and dance, while others avoid dealing with the subject. Despite the controversy, there is a common point which respects the undeniable African heritage embedded in the musical, rhythmic cycles, including the musical instruments such as the *cuíca*, *berimbau*, *caxixi*, and *agogô*. The objective of this study is not to resolve this academic dispute, but bring to light the musical elements inherited from Africa, with a particular emphasis on its probable cultural origins among the Bantu from the Democratic Republic of Congo (henceforth referred as the DRC or simply, Congo). This study will also analyze its mutation process and persistence as a result of various psychological and sociological cultural phenomena, and its continuity in the Americas.

It is impossible to deal with the musical element introduced to Brazilian culture by Bantu people without considering the cultural diversity existing among the numerous societies belonging to the same cultural origin, although this is purely a linguistic phenomenon. For the sake of this study, when we use the term "Bantu," we are referring to the group of societies that occupied the ancient Kingdom of Kongo during the beginning of transatlantic slaving in the sixteenth century. In other words, these societies occupied the Congo River Valley and the area that we define as the "cultural interaction zone," which extends across both sides of the Congo-Angola border. Here we exclude Gabon and Mayombe, as during this period they were organized into autonomous nations.d

Among the musical elements detected to have Bantu origin are the presence of four pulses and sixteen pulses timelines, respectively:

Rhythmic patterns are a characteristic of *samba*, *caxixi*, and *capoeira* music and bring to mind many enigmas, particularly those related to the definition of the so-called Bantu slave group. Such enigmas are revitalized by the fact that in Congo, these musical elements belong to the musical culture of a society. (In this study, "Congo" and "Kongo" are used interchangeably to refer both to a region and a composite people.) This society occupies an area in the countryside—away from the area where the Portuguese empire conducted three centuries of transatlantic slaving activities. On the other hand, you can see that the participation of the members of the Luba society in transatlantic slaving would be sufficient to justify the presence of these elements in Brazilian popular music. But an examination of the reports on Portuguese transatlantic slaving activities in the Kingdom of Kongo reveals that in the absence of appropriate conditions and means, most regions—among them the Luba—in the interior of the Congo River Basin could not be exploited.

Starting from this premise, our first hypothesis will be formulated in the following terms: there should be a strong cultural link between independent states (Angola, Benguela, Congo, Loango), constituents of the first Kongo empire which reached its apogee in the sixteenth century, among the various groups of the Congo Basin, and among the members of the second Kongo empire assimilated by conquests. The Bantu societies had a common origin, a fact corroborated by shared foundational concepts found in the available linguistic evidence. This cultural unification was a consequence of various activities like commercial exchanges, contacts in the battlefields, and migration that occurred after the aforementioned movement of the first Kongo Empire.

Upon observing the use of musical elements among the Luba, the symbolic value traditionally assigned to these elements can be easily understood by their role. Along with the extra-musical elements (props, place, customs, etc.), the symbolic value constitutes the expression of total invocation by which the musical elements are identified and from which they derive their existence. Among the Bakongo, whose friction drum must have reached the Americas, or among the Kuba, which had assimilated its use, the instrument was equipped with a mystical meaning manifested at the ceremony to represent the voices of the ancestors or the sound of the totemic animal of society. In Brazil, it is clear that with the creation of modern Congo music in the beginning of the colonial period, among the camps of workers emerging around

INTRODUCTION

the headquarters of economically exploitative companies, there was the persistence of an organological structure of musical instruments and cycles of rhythmic patterns, and the sacrifice of their cultural values.

With the above in mind, we now discuss our second hypothesis. The traditional values associated the musical elements for which Bantu societies in the Congo Basin held eminently important became part of the popular cultural expression in Brazil and must have occurred due to a crisis in the core of the individual or collective existence, in Bantu terms, thus affecting these elements and their carriers.

At this time, it is possible to present a third hypothesis. Not being rhythmic patterns, the reason for the predominance of the four pulses timeline at the beginning of the creation of the *samba* and the sixteen pulses timeline in more recent dates are absolutely found in the body of musical elements considered common among the members of the transplanted societies; and here we recognize the presence of enslaved Africans coming from other cultural-linguistic families, such as those from Sudanic Africa. Why has the *cuíca* (an indirect friction drum that shares principles with another indirect friction drum known in Portugal during the period of Atlantic slavery) maintained the Bantu organological structure in Brazil but adapted to Portuguese Christmas usage and carnival demonstrations? Are the persistence and the continuity of these musical elements in Brazil functional, as Herskovits has suggested? Would it even be logical to think about persistence as a simple expression of the "necessity of existence"? To some extent, this is a pragmatic question, suggesting an answer of the same nature.

Stressing the interdisciplinary nature of studying popular music, Philip Tagg writes, "No analysis of musical discourse can be considered complete without consideration of social, psychological, visual, gestural, ritual, technical, historical, economic, and linguistic aspects relevant to the genre, function, style, (re-) performance situation, and listening attitude connected with the sound event being studied."[4] This holistic orientation, continues Tagg, helps the scholar discover the interrelationships among the various systems and subsystems in a community or program under study through an emphasis on the contextualization. In other words, a holistic approach will be applied in this study in order to capture a full understanding of all factors interacting with the conception, transmission, and reception of the object study.[5] John Blacking and David Coplan express a similar posture.[6]

Although not defined by scientific methods in ethnomusicology, the first question seems to be determined by the nature of the last. The search for an appropriate methodology in ethnomusicology can be deduced from the interests and the varied contributions made by numerous authors. Many of these contributions can be enumerated, but in spite of the different approaches (e.g., anthropological, bimusicality, sociological, acculturation, transculturation), similarities can be found. These similarities are as follows:

1. Analysis of the music as a product of human behavior in society;

2. Analysis of the music itself (as a phenomenon); and

3. Analysis of music within the context of the phenomena of their creators' society. In other words, music is an expressive synthesis of socioeconomic, political, religious, and other factors, which influence the biotope within which humans live. Therefore, the musical elements mean nothing when isolated; they need the corroboration of extra-musical activities.

In short, although the focus of our study is music as a product of human behavior, our empirical attention is given to studies about the phenomena influencing the human behavior of musical creativity. Mantle Hood has referred to these phenomena as creators of musical consensus. Among them, Hood mentions three interrelated categories of consensus:

1. Musical, including the interaction of musicians and composers with teachers, theorists, critics, entrepreneurs and others involved in the creation of music.

2. Cultural, composed of any group involved in the process of cultural expression outside of musical creation itself.

3. Social, consisting of groups with their own interests, such as religious orders, military branches, government, political elites, and social classes.

These determinants are identified by Roger Bastide as causalities, which he differentiates as either an "external causality," the action exerted by the social mean, or an "internal causality," the transforming action that the individual psyche stimulates. These are the same terms that Marxists call "dynamic."

Our interdisciplinary methodology is rooted in an anthropological method that defines the cultural affinities and the means of dissemination of cultural elements among the Bantu societies in the Congo Basin; an historical method that outlines the cultural migration in the basin, its involvement in slave activities, and the likely route of internal migration in Brazil during and after transatlantic slaving, leading to the current agglomeration in specific areas. The same method clarifies the possible date for the creation of Brazilian musical forms; a comparative study of music identified by staged musical elements with their Bantu origin; and a sociological methods, by which problems related to transplantation of cultural practices and its resistance, mutation, and continuity in the Americas are solved when analyzed within their bearers' cultural context. These complementary methods are not applied in a specific order, but are introduced when needed to provide an understanding or clarify the facts. Their pragmatic nature will be revealed during the course of our discussion.

It is in this line of thought that our bibliographic and field research was guided. The published sources revealed a lack of specific attempts to identify elements of African culture found in Brazilian life and culture with their African cultural origins. The majority of the published literature speaks in a general way about these elements. What specifics it has are geared toward studies in religious syncretism and linguistic influence. During fieldwork research in Congo and in Brazil, using observation and cultural-musical participation, several of our hypotheses began to crystallize and much of what was found in the literature proved to be contradictory. In this sense, our subject choice and the uniqueness of our contribution are not in question.

In order to avoid repetition of the musical presentations, the transcripts included in this book are qualitatively different, in that they are selected from the Bantu playlists (Luba and Congo) and Brazilian popular music in order to illustrate our main arguments.

PART I
REDEFINITION

CHAPTER 1

A REDEFINITION OF THE
ENSLAVED BANTU PEOPLES

When Diogo Cão's expedition reached the mouth of the Congo River, more than half a century still had to pass for Bahia to be found in 1549 and more than three decades since enslaved Africans were transported to Portugal.[7] Since then, numerous writers have offered descriptions about the nature of the Kingdom of Kongo, the homeland from which many enslaved Africans came to Brazil. From these writers we can see that the Kingdom of Kongo, with which the Portuguese Empire maintained trade relations, differed in borders from that which prospered before the sixteenth century.

In 1867, Louis Jacolliot described the geography of the kingdom as encompassing "the entire part of the west African coast between the Equator and 19°S latitude, from Gabon to Cabo Frio," and inclusive of the states of Kongo, Angola and Benguela.[8] In his *Nouvelle Géographie Universelle*, published twelve years after Jacolliot, Elisée Reclus described the same boundaries and confirms that this kingdom stretched from Gabon to the Kwanza River. Georges Balandier, referencing seventeenth century Dutch compiler Olfert Dapper, makes a clear separation between the first and the second kingdom: "It is a political system widely spread on the two margins of the river, which is well described as extending from the north of the present-day Gabon, because the vassal kingdom of Loango reached the cape of Santa Catarina... and to the south beyond the margins of the Kwanza; extending to the Bateke plateau and Kwango River from the ocean..." (see Map I).[9]

The states were a conglomeration of societies whose political organization was characterized by a federation of small autonomous republics and not monarchical states. When they arrived at the end of the fifteenth century, the Portuguese noticed that "the whole territory—in the lower part of the river on the two sides and a large part of the southern plateau—acknowledged the power of a sovereign who resided in the city. The city was known as Mbanza Kongo [later renamed Saõ Salvador by the Portuguese, after converting king Afonso I to Christianity], and that all the chiefs paid the sovereign [called the *manikongo*] regular taxes. The Portuguese government only had the work on replacing the kingdom's ruler to gradually transform the African empire into a subordinate African kingdom."[10]

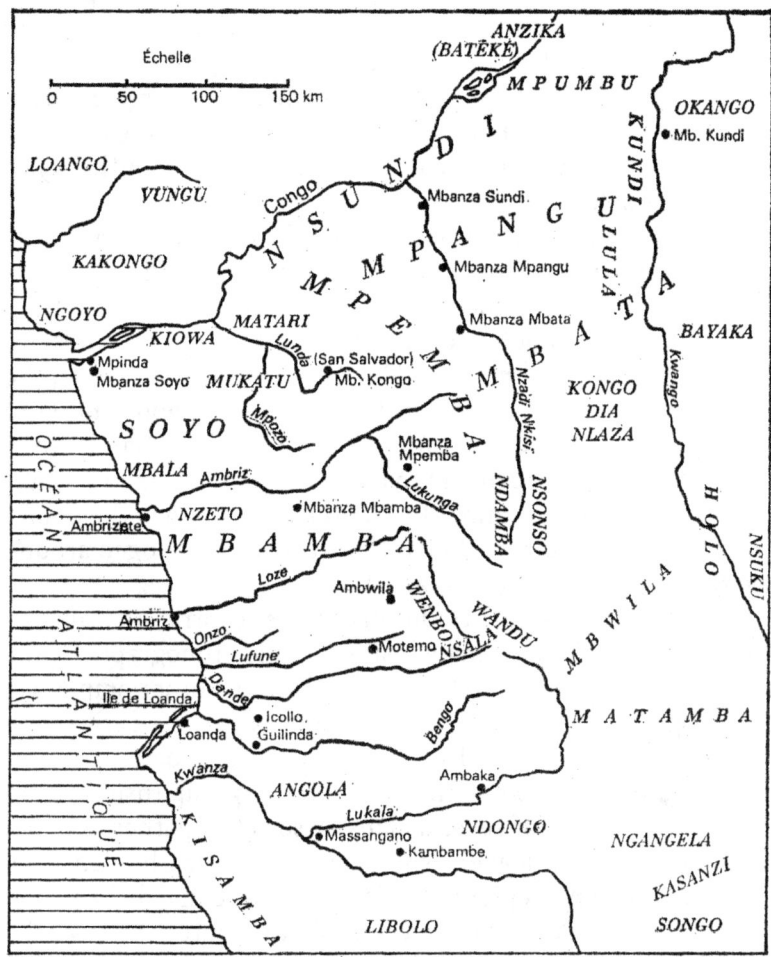

Map I: Congo and its neighbors. Reproduced from Georges Balandier, La Vie Quotidienne au royaume de Kongo (1965), p. 12.

In the sixteenth century the Kingdom of Kongo would suffer the first displacement among its member states, leading to the creation of four separate nations. Jacolliot notes, "The Portuguese intervention ended by bringing the empire of the Kongo to ruin. Later, the wars of religious propaganda as well as the slave hunters' expedition pitted one province against the other and each society regained its independence."[11] Hence we find different names to identify enslaved Africans, according to their ports of embarkation, Dieudonné Rinchon, among others writing about the transatlantic slaving activities of Pierre-Ignace-Lievin Van Alstein, devotes an entire volume to the slaving region from Cape Lopes up to the mouth of the Congo River, where enslaved Africans called Mayombe, Bateke, and Bakamba from the Nyari Valley were sold.[12]

The Kingdom of Kongo, at the time of Portuguese arrival, "actually decreased [in size] and the Congo River outlined its real northern border....To the south, the Bengo separated it from the Kingdom of Angola. To the east, the Kwango continues to represent its approximate limit."[13] For historian C. R. Boxer, the "Kingdom of Kongo can be considered as the region limited to the north by Zaire [Congo] River, to the south by Dande River, to the west by the ocean and to the east by the Kwango River."[14] Historian Jan Vansina and other writers also confirm the boundaries of the Kingdom of Kongo that reached its apogee around the sixteenth century (see Map II).[15]

According to the oral traditions of west central African societies and the records used by historians and ethnographers, the creation of this empire did not differ from the other empires of the Congo Basin, for example, the Luba as per the description of Verhulpen and R. P. Cole.[16] The main creation pattern can be summed up in the command of a powerful group (usually composed by members of several clans or societies gathered under the command of a leader, whose origin remains hidden from their vassal) being deployed in clans that were invaded and conquered.[17] In Congo around the fourteenth century, a powerful warrior and his followers had invaded and captured an area inhabited by the Ambundu society. Many members of that society were reduced to enslavement, some assimilated and others fled to the south. After its establishment there, the kingdom was expanded, with subsequent invading expedition being "made up by people coming from the country."[18] Among these people from the interior were the Kuba, Lunda, Yaka, and others, whose importance is related to the means of cultural dissemination in the Congo Basin.

Vansina tells us that, "From its capital Wene, lands were dominated that later came to be known as the provinces of Mpemba and Soyo. Two kingdoms to the east, Mpangu and Mbata which seem to have pre-existed, were incorporated."[19] According to this description, we can conclude with Balandier that "certain territories encrusted in it—Wembo, Wando, Nkusu, Matari—and the peripheral regions such as the Ambundu province, were more dependent than areas subordinate to the direct control of the Congo's king."[20] The highest plateau of the entire kingdom was the capital city where the *manikongo* resided, traditionally known as the *Iron Smith King* (blacksmith) and by the Portuguese as the "Christian" king.

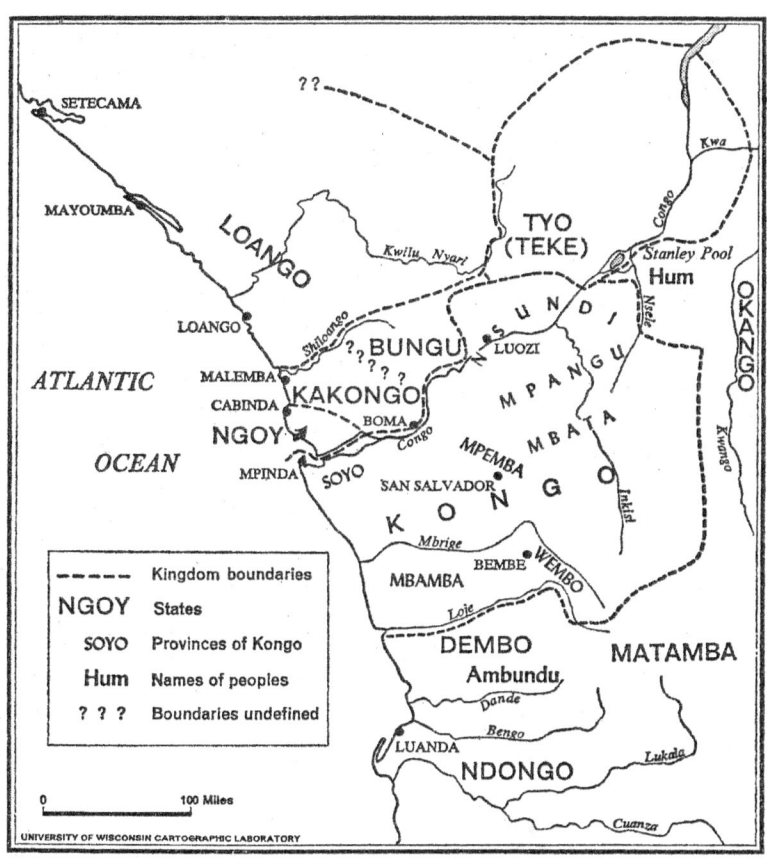

Map II: The Kingdom of Kongo in sixteenth century. Reproduced from Jan Vansina, Kingdoms of the Savanna (1966), p. 39.

The reports that proudly describe the capital of the kingdom are too numerous to be listed. But to give readers an idea of its geography, Cuvelier provides one such account: "Rising to an altitude of 559 meters, the mountain forms a plateau of seven kilometers in length in the north-south direction. It bows from the west to the valley. To a distance of one kilometer runs the sinuous Luezi [Luwozi] River, affluent of the Lunda that makes the neighboring region quite pleasant and fertile. The inhabitants could establish beautiful plantations there. On the plateau itself, there are two sources of clear water. The place was always considered to be a very salutary land."[21] For Olfert Dapper, the city was located on the highest mountain in the land because from the landing port of Pinda to the Congo, it took ten days to reach the city and the province of Pemba. This province was located in the heart of the kingdom and it was the head of all the other provinces, the origin of the ancient kingdoms.[22]

A panoramic view can be described for the first and the second Kingdom of Kongo. The first was a union of independent states and the second was forged from conquests and expanded by temporary adhesion such as in the case of the Kuba, or permanent adhesions such as in the case of the Bayombe. All of these took place during the sixteenth century, reported as the "period of large migrations." It is in the last kingdom where the Portuguese empire established Christianity. They started diplomatic and trade relations with the royal family and educational programs for the royal court. On the other hand, this is the same kingdom that the Portuguese empire would help to destroy by arming the Yaka in 1568 after the battle of the Kingdom against the Tyo (Teke) in the year before.[23]

The political and geographical borders should be viewed as if they were vertically emerging from a cultural imaginary plane. This cultural level is from the "Bantu," who occupied, before the creation of the first and the second kingdoms, the entire central part of Africa, including the area covered by both. The generic name "Bantu" was given to a group of black African languages studied in 1862 by Wilhelm Bleek, who noticed that the word used for people—*mu*-ntu (pl. *ba*-ntu)—was the same in the 2,000 studied languages. The expansion of the Bantu peoples that led to the occupation of close to one-third of the continent, and the origins of the kingdoms they spawned, is still a subject of controversy. Scholars from different research fields emphasize one or another aspect, such as the advent of edible Malaysian plants, linguistic stock, metallurgical knowledge, agricultural techniques and the cattle.[24] George Murdock, an anthropologist, based his hypothesis on the same linguistic evidence as linguist Joseph Greenberg to demonstrate the region from which the Bantu originated. According to Greenberg, "The languages of the Bantu as a group, in spite of its wide distribution, constitute one of the seven branches of the subdivision of macro-Bantu subfamily Bantuide from Negroid race. The other six branches of macro-Bantu, each one closely coordinated with the Bantu as a whole, are confined to a small area near the border of Cameroon-Nigeria."[25] In studies from 1963 to 1972, the question was handled under a macroscopic angle showing the similarities between the languages of the Bantu and the Sudanese. Greenberg emphasizes, "The Bantu will not be enough to constitute a single genetics subfamily...but it belongs to one of the subfamilies... Benue-Cross or Semi-Bantu."[26] Based on this evidence, Murdock agreed with Greenberg that on "linguistic grounds, it is impossible that the Bantu may have come from any other place. The original country of the Bantu should have been immediately adjacent to the territory of those who speak other languages of macro-Bantu. This was in the mountainous region of Cameroon and in a strip of low land connecting this with the opposite coast to the island of Fernando Pó. It must have covered a very restricted area because the remaining Bongo hunters provided testimonies about the ancient [Batwa peoples] occupation just a few kilometers to the south and east."[27]

About the Bantu expansion, Murdock compares the diffusion of Malaysian banana culture, taro, and yam, which were established on the Azaniana coast in East Africa around 60 CE with the Sudanese agricultural technique developed in their plantations in the savanna region and the rainy equatorial forest region (the habitat of the Batwa peoples) to which only the Bantu were adapted. He says, "Once the Bantu ancestors borrowed these edible plants, its expansion to the south and to the east became inevitable."[28] This migratory movement, according to the author, occurred during the last 2,000 years: "We cannot be totally wrong if we set the first century as a probable period for the beginning of the Bantu expansion. Without a doubt, a route developed within the tropical forest toward the south along the Atlantic coast and it seems to have been followed by emigrants from the lower part of the homeland of Bantu."[29]

This hypothesis seems to be confirmed by the discoveries published by Cheikh Anta Diop in his *Nation Nègres et Cultures* (1954), in which the author states that the black man's origin in the Nile valley in Egypt existed at least until the fourth dynasty of the pharaohs (2,600 BCE). After this period, their power and cultural strength became ephemeral due to the infiltration of foreign culture. This, according to the author, has caused the loss of empire and the beginning of the movement south (probably in the region of Cameroon highlands, by the group that will be known until today as the Bantu). Writing in the same line of thought, Raymond A. Dart shows in his book *Racial Origins* that the ancestors of the Bantu participated in commercial activities with the Roman and Greek merchants who traded (45 CE) in the Indian Ocean.[30] Basing his findings on an ancient account, Periplus of the Erythrean Sea, Dart continues that these merchants had contact with the Ausanitica coast from Azânia (a term referreing, at various times, to the east African coast, southeast Africa and, more recently, South Africa). From Africa, describes the author, the Roman and Greek merchants garnered ivory, rhinoceros horns, tortoise-shell, palm oil, and enslaved Africans in exchange for spears, hatchets, daggers, punches, glass, wine, and wheat.

Dart concludes that "We do not know when the Bantu gained sufficient numerical strength, political organization and knowledge to become independent of the imports of spears, axes, etc. from the merchants on the coast. This happened in the first five centuries of the Christian era and they went down in large quantities to the east of Africa..."[31] Later, the same author, offers a more conclusive statement regarding the migratory movement of Bantu to their current settlements: "After destroying the Sabean power, the Abyssinians were able to retain their own independence and prevent the flow of the Bantu from the north to the east. However, due to the relaxed control of the Sabean on the east coast port and in the gold producer belt of southern Africa, the Khoisan peoples from that territory became an easy prey of Bantu who had moved to the south since the end of the sixth century. Probably we are not very far from truth if we place the first great migration of Bantu to the south around this period."[32]

The migratory movement to the south was partially refuted by Malcolm Guthrie, who devoted most of his efforts to the comparative study of Bantu languages. In his article, "Contributions from Comparative Bantu Studies to the Prehistory of Africa," he assumes the isoglosses (lines connecting points corresponding to the identical percentage in relation to common Bantu) delineated the common Bantu nuclear area covered in herbs from the south of the Congo forest which extends between the Zambezi and Congo rivers. Guthrie speculated, according to archaeologist Merrick Posnansky, the proto-Bantu developed in this area, where the expansion started. Plunging into their concerns, Guthrie agrees partially with Murdock when he admits that there were two dialects in proto-Bantu—the east and the west—containing in its vocabulary about 60 percent of terms from closely related dialects. In proto-Bantu, Gurthrie observed that words such as *fishing, canoe, rowing,* and *forge* were commonly used and the word for *forest* proto-Bantu designates as the *fourré* and not the great forest. Using these observations, he concludes that the people who spoke the proto-Bantu would have, prior to their dispersion, known how to work with iron and they lived south of the great forest itself and commonly used boats and waterways.

The linguistic opinion of Guthrie is not accepted by other scholars such as Christopher Ehret, who agreed with Greenberg that the first Bantu lived 3,000 years ago in the forest where they were farmers and fishermen. But after the description given by Sutton, who remarked that the word *cow* in Bantu languages was taken from the language of Central Sudan suggesting the imitation of livestock breeding, he deduced that the breeders preceded the farmers. Ehret agrees with the division of the proto-Bantu and their land of origin made by Guthrie when he suggests that the region around Lake Tanganyika was strategic for the subsequent dispersion of the eastern group of proto-Bantu, because it was ideally suited for both the sorghum crop and livestock farming.[33] But later Ehret "also noted that the words that designate the hoe and sorghum in proto-Bantu languages are derived from the Central Sudan, which leads us to think of the two events: a social interaction between the people of Nilo-Saharan and the ancestors of Bantu; and the dissemination of a practiced agriculture to the south by means of hoe (metal) as well as of sorghum crop, and this was in the direction of countries occupied by Bantu."[34] This leads us to accept the emphasis of Ehret about the eastern homeland of the Bantu, as suggested by Guthrie, when he specifies the dissemination of agricultural practice and the sorghum crop to the south.

Basing his conclusions on the age of fossils, whose discoveries were published in articles by Jacques Nenquin and Guthrie, David Birmingham argues, "The linguistic evidence parallel to the historical importance of Luba is in high correlation with the Luba language with a hypothetical proto-Bantu vocabulary that I think may have been used by the Bantu before their dispersion to the south of Africa. The correlation of other Bantu languages decreases with its distance to the Luba."[35] Birmingham also thinks the Bantu might have spread from an origin in Katanga.[36]

We may have a preference for one or the other hypotheses put forward in the present discussion—all trying to solve the enigma of the cultural and linguistic origin of Bantu and their respective migratory movement that led to their rootedness in one-third of Africa. Independent of our preference, the dispersed Bantu societies shared a common origin and had values, standards, practices, etc., as common cultural elements. Yet the respective migratory route (still a controversial academic subject) is gathered from writings on the divergence of the Bantu, and referred to as "common cultural denominators." In other words, subsequent contacts (e.g., fusion, meetings, commercial ventures, battles) which occurred in their migratory routes forced the modification or the reinterpretation of these "common cultural denominators," thereby differentiating one group or society from the other. You can then estimate using this chain of thought that each group had shaped a cultural focus from the "cultural common denominators." These were ideological and materialistic concepts—ones that govern and influence the manifestation of human behavior, including artistic expression, myths, social organization, kinship systems, and so on.

Concrete examples of the variety of this same cultural practice can be observed between societies of the Congo Basin in their social organization in matters of inheritance, succession, and social status. While the Bakongo, the Yombe, and the Luena are from a maternal line, the Luba and the Songye practice the double descent. And among the Kuba, in exchange for a great legacy through marriage, some of the children were separated from maternal groups to become members of the paternal lineage.[37] More examples of this variety are also found in religious practices of the same societies of Congo where, according to Tempels in his book *Bantu Philosophy* (1956), the vital force of *muntu* (living force or causal agent in all humans) is their belief in a supreme being who transcends the entire structural organization.[38] We can see, however, varieties in the interpretation of the global cultural belief such as it exists among the Kuba. For them, the belief in life after death is not the same as their neighboring Luba. They believe in a life after death, which is guaranteed by an act of naming children with the spirit of the deceased who reincarnates after death. And before being born in human form for the second time, the soul first lives in another form (such as animals, plants, etc.) in nature.

As far as the Kingdom of Kongo is concerned, studies by historians and ethnographers have shown that long before the arrival of Europeans in the sixteenth century, the societies met in several warehouses for temporary trade. According to Balandier, "It is in the Mpumbu contact (Stanley Pool) that relations and the trade with the people of the North were established, especially the Ba-Teke."[39] Another of these trade warehouses were described by Louis de Saint Moulin in Kitambo (a region of Kinshasa), located towards the northeast, in the region of the Teke or Bateke peoples. According to Saint Moulin, the societies involved in trade were the Bakongo, the Bazombo (Luanda), the Bateke (occupants of the region), and the Lari and Yombe on the other side of the Congo River.[40]

The importance of temporary meetings can be considered from various aspects. From a historical point of view, these meetings have confirmed that there was a certain degree of peaceful exchange between the participating societies, thus facilitating trade. From a socio-anthropological perspective, these meetings have resulted in the exchange and the crystallization of cultural elements (such as arts, harvest celebrations, linguistic features, medicinal plants, etc.). They also established a basis for the common cultural traits found between the Congo River and Angola. In the nineteenth century, these encounters forced the creation of an expressional language—a good example of which is Lingala, a langue arising out of the need for communication during trade--composed basically of words derived from the linguistic communities of the societies involved.

In the rest of the Congo Basin, the fifteenth and sixteenth centuries were a period of large migratory movements; a period during which the families were divided into autonomous groups, and a period that saw the establishment of new empires and the expansion of borders by means of conquest. Ethnographic studies have been published on these societies and anthropology students at the National University of Congo has produced new evidence by means of cultural similarities, artistic expressions, etc., for the establishment of cultural origins, affinities, and their likely routes through the basin. On the other hand, valuable pioneering works such as *Baluba et Balubaises du Katanga*; the works of Verhulpen and R. P. Colle; Vansina's *Le royaume Kuba* and *Kingdoms of the Savanna*; and G. Balandier, *La Vie Quotidienne au Royaume de Kongo du XVI au XVIII Siecle* should not be forgotten. While the first two are committed to solving the problems concerning the origin of Luba (their empires and evolution before the Europeans arrived), the third does the same with the empire of Kuba, and the fourth deals with the movements of the societies in the basin, referencing the historical reports of the largest empires in the area. Finally, these authors remind us of the important sociological facts about daily life in the Kingdom of Kongo and among those within its dominion and among its neighbors.

For the Luba, the state of Bena Kalundwe in the Lubilash River was infiltrated and conquered by the Songye coming from the north. Having Bena Kalundwe, Songye established the first Luba Empire in Katanga (Shaba) and started the Bakongolo dynasty.[41] As David Birmingham notes, "This empire spread over a wide area and probably survived for several centuries. During this time, their monarchy—with successive paternal lines—had taken root among the Luba and was adopted by subsequent invaders and dynasties that had spread to the neighboring states."⁴² With the killing of Kongolo Mwana in the battlefield by his nephew Kalala llunga (who became the new ruler), considerable turmoil in the empire led to the migration of the followers of Kongolo to the banks of the Kasai River—hence they are called "Luba Kasai."⁴³ Thus the Luba or Baluba evolved along the lines of the "population of the first empire founded by Kongolo, the second empire founded by Ilunga Mbili (Kalala llunga), the Kingdom of Kikondja founded by the descendants of Bombwi Mbili and all regions won later by the Luba."⁴⁴

From the writings of Verhulpen on the Luba and of other scholars on the Bolia within the tropical rainforest of the Congo, it can be deduced that the internal developments of these societies allowed for the expansion of borders and increase in population. More important, these developments were a channel for cultural fusion, with the conquerors imposing their culture on the conquered, and in return the conquered mixing the newly adopted culture with elements of their own. This occurred in the vast empire of Luba, which extended from Maniema in the south, Shaba and Lubilash in the west, to the Lake Tanganyika and Lake Moero in the east. From a cultural point of view, we are forced to agree with Birmingham that these empires (Luba, Kongo, and Bolia) lasted for a time which was enough to homogenize a lifestyle (including myths, family systems, linguistic and artistic expression, etc.); basic traits of this lifestyle are found in different interpretions by the clan and their derivatives in respective geographical areas.

It would seem the Bena Lunda are also Baluba, since they were a part of the first Luba empire of Kunga-Songye that was later conquered by the Luba hunter Kibinda Ilunga and his followers.⁴⁵ The consequences of the westward migration of a Lunda group known as the Imbangala, guided by Kinguri-Kya-Banguela, can be studied in the valuable analysis by Birmingham.⁴⁶ At this moment we are not interested in clarifying the confusing surrounding the two distinctly separate groups of completely different origins, but the nature of the movement to the west of Imbangala, that is, the important types of contact that were forged during the journey to the west whose duration is still unknown. In the works of Birmingham it is found that the group, composed of followers of Kinguri and other leaders of the Lunda, was forced to leave the land occupied by the Luba invaders and migrated to the west under the leadership of Kinguri-Kya-Bangela somewhere between late fifteenth century and the early sixteenth century, certainly before 1575. From time to time, the main contingent was divided into small invasive groups whose routes were dispersed; they brought strong members of the conquered groups to the periphery of their camps. The author characterizes them as "terrible people"—they practiced cannibalism and never raised their own children. "To increase their ranks," wrote Birmingham, "they recruited strong adolescents from the conquered people and initiated the livelihoods of Imbangala."[47] The Jaga (Yaka), another nomadic group in Central Africa who had similar characteristics, had the strength of around 16,000 in the field, but only twelve or fourteen men and fifteen women out of them were originally Yaka.[48]

After settling in the Kwango-Kwanza region for some time, the first contingent joined the Lunda leaders who followed the route of Kinguri to escape the Luba. Before the death of Kinguri, according to the seventeenth century Italian Capuchin missionary Giovvanni Cavazzi, the forces of the Imbangala joined with those of the Yaka and invaded the Kingdom of Kongo around 1560.[49] They temporarily expelled both the king and the Portuguese who lived in the court. After Kinguri died in Angola around 1563, the Imbangala stopped following a single leader and split into autonomous groups. One of these groups, headed by the Kasanje, went to Luanda and expelled the Ambundu, who were in a contact with the Portuguese on the island of the same name. After conquering Luanda, the group established contact with the Portuguese traders and slave merchants. From 1575 to the late seventeenth century, the Imbangala occupied both sides of the Congo-Angola border, which ran along the tributaries of the Kasai River. On the other hand, the Bakongo conquered the Yaka. This resulted in the division of the original group into two main groups: The stronger group got absorbed by the conquerors and the rebel group took refuge on the banks of the Kwango River, where they preserved their culture.

Regarding the Imbangala and the Yaka, there is enough evidence to believe that certain common cultural elements got established in the Congo Basin due to migration. These elements culturally united the Kingdom of Kongo with the rest of the basin and also spread into Angola. The Imbangala or the Yaka not only spread their original values to the coastal region but also assimilated other cultural elements into their own. Striking examples of the Luba-Lunda culture are found in the sedimented cultures of Congo and Ambundu with which they were in contact.

According to Vansina, it can be stated that the Yaka had cultural links with the Luba-Lunda, probably the Imbangala. The reason is that all the unique features of their culture can be found in the culture of the Luba-Lunda, which no longer exists in the area of the lower Congo.[50] He says that this cultural evidence confirm the testimonies of the seventeenth century authors and that the name of one of the Yaka, named Kalandula, is very close to a Lunda title, Kalandala.[51]

A deeper into the cultural history of the basin—before, during and after the sixteenth century, the great migratory period—reveals other means of dissemination and cultural unification. There is also a division in the group of families such as that of the Imbangala and the Luba, the Mongo, and the Tetela, or the Kuba. On this issue E. Cornet (1972), blindly copying Vansina, says that these societies are an agglomeration of groups having various origins. But probing deeper, according to a meticulous illustration of Mputu in his study on the origin of the Kuba, Cornet admits these societies were groups of families and their followers who were once displaced.

Speculations about the origins of the Kuba hold more importance. After all the evidence suggests that their culture dispersed and left their footprints on the cultures of those with whom they made contact, and took from them elements they thought appropriate for their own development, and this contact brought both diverse versions of the original culture, and the union of elements having diverse backgrounds. This union resulted in the development of a cultural stock between the groups who were looking for a new cultural expression.

William Fagg undoubtedly suggests that the Kuba absorbed the artistic style of the Congo and a migratory movement likely ensued. He writes, "It is very clear that a large part of the art of the Bakuba was born in the Kingdom of Kongo under the rule of the great king Shanaba Bolongongo, around 1600. Under him, most of the inventions and social progress took place, including the custom of carving a "portrait-statue" for each sovereign. After his death, these statues served as an important part of ritual ceremonies; they are similar to the funerary statues or Shabti of Bakongo."[52] The migratory route of Kuba can be traced in the geographical distribution of the *tshihumba* (Congo guitar) from the right bank of the Kasai River, in the lower Congo, to the western Kasai.

After the Bantu dispersed throughout Africa, other contacts (battles, temporary trade meetings, migration, recruitment, etc.) contributed greatly to the establishment of the "common cultural denominators" in the basin. That contact, which took place between the societies in the Congo Basin during the period of transatlantic slaving with Brazil, resulted in the crystallization of cultural centers. The same contacts were also responsible for the transmission of traditional elements from interior areas to the coastal region. Among these traditional elements is musical expression, the subject of our interest.

Although observations made during different periods have not been able to distinguish the nature of cultural changes (e.g., profound and radical versus superficial or temporary), the fact is that these "common cultural denominators" are perceived as different interpretations of the cultural life—from the Kasai region to the lower Congo, through the southern region which is the current Kikwit. If we draw an imaginary horizontal line from Lubumbashi to Benguela near the ocean, we would find strong cultural similarities which exist in the area covered by this line with the Angolan territory and the area in Congo which extends from the lower Congo, through the southern region (i.e., the lands of the Kuba, Luba) until Shaba (see Map III). Fagg artistically confirms our definition of the cultural interaction through the visual arts among all societies of the Bakongo complex (which includes the Bayombe and the Bavili situated on the right bank of the Congo River), Cabinda, and Angola, and amongst the Basuku, the Bayaka, and the Bambala in the Kwango-Kwilu Basin. According to Fagg, the Bapende shared much with societies of the Kwango-Kwilu Basin on one hand and with the Bakuba (on the west bank of the Kasai River) on the other hand.[53] These similarities are not due to the societies being Bantu cultural groups, but due to their continuous contact with each other before the arrival of the Portuguese.

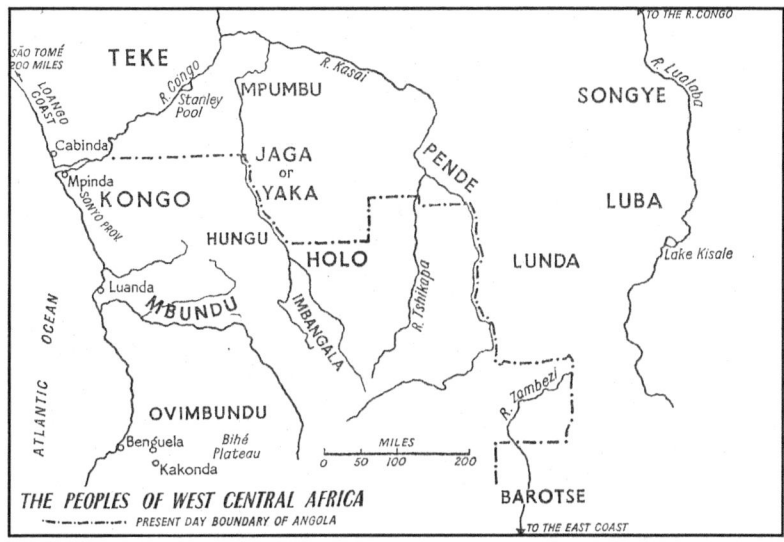

Map III: The Peoples of West Central Africa

Much confirmating evidence to support the idea of cultural convergences can be found in the central concept of the Bantu family. These family structures influenced social organization, and religious, political, economic, and artistic systems for both the maternal and the paternal line. These determinant cultural values can be perceived in the Bantu philosophy of existence—the *muntu* incorporate a philosophy of life after death manifested in the name of the child and also attempts to incorporate personal merit—that gives each individual a dual identity. The first identity is the "spiritual identity" depending on the ancestor's name the individual carries. In this sense, the emphasis placed on the family lineage, and the merits of the ancestors. The second is known as the "physical identity," which determines or reflects physical characteristic or phenomena such as the land, mountains, rivers, physical appearance, and forms the main identity of the *muntu*. Each individual in the core family has to function on two levels, which are attributed within this dynamic structure. Some functions are inherited functions, such as those carried out by the family of the deceased person whose name a child bears; and the others are known as "hierarchical roles," determined by the position of the person in the family structure, such as father, twins, uncle, etc.[54]

Although we must not hastily reach conclusions, it seems the participation of interior cultural members in the transatlantic slaving to Brazil was indispensable in the spread of their cultural cultural elements to the Americas. An explanation of this and its related issues can be found in the participation of the Kingdom of Kongo in transatlantic slaving with the Portuguese. Evidence of Bantu cultural traits present in Brazilian life and artistic expression supports the argument on which the first part of our hypothesis is based, but the common cultural denominator detailed already will depend on factors related to the nature of the capture and trade in enslaved Africans by the Portuguese and Dutch in the second Kingdom of Kongo. These factors determine its crystallization, which Maurice Halbwachs called the "collective memory" of two Congo in the Americas.

The relationship between the Portuguese Empire and the Kingdom of Kongo began when Diogo Cão made his second trip to the mouth of the Congo River in 1483 and visited the court of the *manikongo* (ruler) in the capital Mbanza Kongo, some 200 kilometers into the interior. In 1491, Portugal was already sending gifts to the *manikongo*, among which musical "organs" are mentioned.[55] Years later, the relations were even more strengthened, and the existence and activities of missionaries in the kingdom are recorded in several reports. As a result of this interaction, we find names of Portuguese origin integrated into the cultural vocabulary of the Congo. Among others, names such as Ndongala, Ndombasi, Ndompetelo, and Ndomanueno are derived from the Portuguese nobility titles "Dom" preceding the given name of persons such as Dom Gastão, Dom Baptista, Dom Pedro, and Dom Manuel. ("Dom" is the abbreviated version of "Deo optimo maximo," meaning "to God, the best and the greatest.")

During the earlier centuries of African-Portuguese interaction, the members of the royal family in the Kingdom of Kongo were sent to Lisbon to study. But the *manikongo* did not know that he would pay a high price for all the help offered by the Portuguese. The Portuguese king Dom Manuel informed the Kongo king Afonso that all payments should be made with enslaved Africans, copper, or ivory, and that these payments were essential to cover the cost of Afonso's son, the sons of nobles who were studying in Portugal, as well as for the missions.[56] Around 1513, the two kings signed treaties to export enslaved Africans of Congo to the islands of Cape Verde and São Tomé, discovered respectively in 1460 and 1470, and whose importance in transatlantic slaving would only grow with time.

Because of the official status of transatlantic slaving, the Kingdom of Kongo was transformed into a hunting region not only by merchants but also by missionaries in the kingdom. The first caravan of enslaved Africans, who jointly belonged to a priest of the capital and a white market, is mentioned during the war between Afonso and Munza, in the area of Mbundu in the south. The noble of Mbundu was accused of attacking a leader from southern Congo. With this invasion, Afonso brought 400 prisoners, 320 of which were shipped to Portugal and the two archipelagos where the sugarcane plantations were already established. By 1530, the number of enslaved Africans exported from the Mpinda port was estimated between 4,000 and 5,000 per year, without considering those who died before reaching their destinations.

Although the exact date of the introduction of enslaved Africans to Brazil is not known, some speculate based on contemporary reports. "In 1511," writes Malheiro, "King Fernando [of Spain]...took measures to improve the conditions of the natives [Amerindians] and favored the import of slaves from Guinea [western Africa]. He even wanted the slaves to be imported in the colonies, in particular Hispaniola, in great numbers."[57] According to Malheiro, six years later Carlos V [also the King of Spain] extended this practice, and awarded a "patent" to a Flemish nobleman to import 4,000 enslaved Africans annually. With no precise date, Malheiro firmly states that sugarcane cultivation in Brazil was introduced under the captaincy of São Vicente and the imported enslaved Africans worked in them. The author mentions that "the caravel, found by Martin Afonso de Sousa in Bahia in 1531 and taken by him for his service after expelling the slaves, was already employed in this trade."[58] In turn, Birmingham says with certainty that a large number of enslaved Africans were brought for the sugarcane plantations on the island of São Tomé, or for the slave market in Lisbon. But starting from the mid-sixteenth century, a much larger market was developed in the colonies in Brazil.[59]

It is uncertain when enslaved African were introduced in Brazil for the first time; maybe in the beginning of the sixteenth century, but certainly prior to 1575, the year when Portugal changed its interests after opening a new colony in Luanda. The Kingdom of Kongo became the preferred region for slave-hunting. This is due to several factors such as the absence of precious metals in the region, the perceived meekness of its people, and the fact that it is relatively easier to cross the Atlantic Ocean in the direction of Brazil. Comparing Sudanese with the Bantu regions of Africa, Pierre Verger agrees with Luiz Vianna Filho that the nature of both the groups was completely different. Whereas the Bantu were more docile and capable of adaptation, the Sudanese had an attitude of rebellion and insulation.[60] In concert with Verger, Rinchon, writing about the enslaved Africans from the Congo to Central America, writes, "Here were sold the best slaves of Mayombe, the Kongo...black, robust, tireless, which were just as good as the best of our colonies. They are healthy and quiet, accustomed to bondage...their only pleasure is to have tobacco and some bananas, they worked cheerfully, singing and wanting nothing more than this."[61]

Several techniques were employed to acquire enslaved Africans. The most common method was to create a conflict between two surrounding societies. The strongest society sold the captured enemies as enslaved individuals, such as the conflict between the Mbundu and the Congo, or armed a group of invaders such as the Yaka, Imbangala, and the Teke in Congo and Mbundu. Considering the scale of capture, it is next to impossible to estimate the exact number of enslaved Africans captured from a given area, since even those who were captured in the region of Congo were not necessarily sold in their market. The enslaved were branded with the name of the region where they were sold—Congo, Angola, or Mayombe.

It is evident that the activities surrounding slave acquisition were limited until around the latter half of the seventeenth century in the second kingdom (within the Congo Basin). This justifies the concerns and the complaints of the King Afonso of the Kingdom of Kongo with the Holy Crown against the evil that this practice of transatlantic slaving was bringing to his kingdom since 1514, when he lost control of this trade. Tailors, shoemakers, masons, potters, priests, and teachers were all ensnared into the trade, and the situation became disastrous around 1526. Afonso wrote to Portugal complaining about these activities:

> We beg Your Royal Highness not to believe in the evil they say about us; we have no other concerns than their trade, they sell what was unfairly purchased by them, and ruin with their trafficking our kingdom and Christianity—established long time ago and which cost so much sacrifice of your predecessors. To achieve a great faith for the people, the kings and the Catholic principles along with Your Royal Highness have worked together. We are committed to retain it for those who sacrificed. But this commitment is difficult to ensure when the ignorant Europeans merchants have so much fascination that they abandon the God who controls them. The remedy is to abolish these goods, which trap the devil for the sellers and buyers. The attraction for profit and greed leads the people of the country to steal from their compatriots, including theirs and our family members, without considering whether or not they are Christians. They capture, sell, and exchange them.[62]

Failing to convince the Portuguese king or the Holy Crown to intervene and stop the transatlantic slaving that was ruining the Kingdom of Kongo, Afonso went to merchants and suggested new regions of hunting in the lands of the Teke, Hum, and the Mbundu. Whatever steps he took, however, were futile. Instead of decreasing the hunt for enslaved Africans in his kingdom, there was a successive increase of wars and invasions by the Teke, Yaka, and Imbangala around 1560, the latter of which eventually led to the kingdom's collapse. Afonso had a lot of reasons to worry—not because of the transatlantic slaving which he himself organized and directed, but because of the negative effects the trade was bringing to his kingdom. Balandier summarizes this situation and says that the hunting of humans—which was justified by economic greed and which was sanctified and practiced in some way or the other by all the "foreign" societies and their agents—was one of the causes of the destruction of old Kongo. This hunting corrupted social relations and encouraged invasions (*razzias*).[63]

What is known about slave hunting within the Congo Basin is related to Arab participation in the region, which extended from the western margin of Tanganika through Kambambare and Lualaba Valley up to the Congo River. The first Arab merchant in these regions is registered by Cornet (1952) as having established himself in the margins of the Lualaba River, in Maniema (Nyangwe) around 1860. Two years before, it is known that the Arabs had a base in Uvira where they collected the products of their exploration in neighboring regions along the valleys of Eur and Ruzizi. The most important of these Arabs was Hamad bin Muḥammad bin Jumah bin Rajab, known as Tippu Tip. He is recorded as having penetrated into Shaba and reached the kingdom of M'Siri in Bunkeya. But it is important to mention here that enslaved Africans of the country gathered by the Arabs were sold in other markets located on the east coast of Africa, where they were traded and sold to colonies other than Brazil.

The most interior that the Portuguese and their auxiliaries could reach was the land of the Teke, about 400 kilometers from the western coast. It was the location where the Kongo were in frequent contact, via temporary commercial meetings, and where the path was not so difficult to retrace. Other difficulties were the diseases of the forest and the Imbangala of Kasanje, who created obstacles for the Portuguese in order to monopolize the domestic market that came to be known as "Kasanje fair." It would be wrong to think that only members of a coastal society of the kingdom, particularly the Bakongo, formed the group of enslaved Africans known as "Kongo" in its majority. The catchment area for the enslaved extended throughout the kingdom—between Stanley Pool and the Atlantic Ocean, along the coast, extending to the north toward the Ogoué, to the interior of the territories of the Bateke, and east beyond the Kwango River. In other words, the involvement of the interior inhabitants is undetectable.

Returning to the original hypothesis regarding the participation of Bantu peoples in transatlantic slaving in order to justify the presence of their cultural expressions in the Americas raises issues concerning the constitution of the enslaved Africans branded as "Kongo slave" group. Taking into account the crystallization of common cultural features among societies in the Congo Basin through various means (e.g., battlefields, temporary commercial meetings, migration, and assimilation by marriage), the Kongo cultural traits that can be detected in Brazil could have been brought by any one of the societies of the basin; the involvement of its members in transatlantic slaving was not necessary.

Between the dissolution of West Central African societies and their lands and their arrival in the Brazilian slave markets, members of different clans and societies, coming from the kingdom and neighboring regions, had enough time to take a cultural inventory. They found the cultural common elements and crystallized the common features that Maurice Halbwachs named "collective memory." A deeper examination of the Bantu contributions already detectable in Brazilian life reveals more evidence that there is a clear distinction in their nature. This confirms the belief that people's participation in transatlantic slaving was not essential, although they were present, and that members of the coastal regions, who had a major role in assimilating the elements, transplanted their cultural elements to the Americas. On one hand, there is the linguistic influence, which is predominantly Kikongo, or from their neighboring Kimbundu. On the other hand, the predominance of traces of the non-coastal regions in the artistic field is undeniable. While the first can be justified by the great number of members of the Kongo and Mbundu areas to ensure its continuity into the present, the latter makes sense when we consider the cultural unification that occurred before and during transatlantic slaving, especially from the interior to the coastal areas.

Halbwachs distinguishes "individual memory" from "collective memory" as follows: "In the first type, the individual retains an event, culture, myth, etc. that he has experimented with a group and who no longer lives. The second, on the other hand, is a set of multiple points of view about an event, culture, etc. that was retained by the members of a group who had shared their events."[64] While the individual memory depends on the ability of the individual to rebuild alone what he or she shared with a group, the collective memory "spreads as far as possible and reaches the memory of the groups that make it up."[65] In other words, "Whatever be the relation of the individual memory with the collective memory, it is in the core of the first that the second takes place."

Although the main concern of this chapter is to reveal the constitution of the collective group of enslaved Africans branded as "Kongo," many groups formed this collective. Their arrival in Brazil extends for three centuries—from the second half of the sixteenth century until the end of the last quarter of the nineteenth century. Each one of these groups of enslaved Africans from Congo was certainly formed under different conditions. Among the conditions, which in essence are responsible for facilitating the consolidation of collective memory, is the time that the captives spent together and the nature of the activities mentioned above.

After the analysis of various processes and techniques used by the Portuguese to acquire enslaved Africans, Boxer says, "These *pombeiros* (slave agents) stayed a long time in the country, one to two years, before sending to the coast or bringing with them five or six hundred slaves."[66] This indicated how difficult it became to capture enslaved Africans with time and how they started hunting in the region's interior. At the coast, enslaved Africans were housed in baracks while waiting for the ship's arrival. In some occasions, many died during this period, which followed a long walk from the interior. Boxer writes, "Usually they arrived from the country in terrible conditions, after walking hundreds of kilometers with almost no food."[67] Indeed, as Birmingham notes, "The number of slaves captured would have been bigger but they were not, because the rate of mortality during the walk to Mpinda and waiting for the ship was long."[68]

At the coast, to ensure the quality of their human commodities, the Portuguese gave the best medical attention they could to the wounded, the weak, and the sick. They also took care to maintain enslaved Africans' healthy weight during the waiting period, which lasted six to eight months, before being shipped across the Atlantic. In the words of Boxer, "the Portuguese took great care in fattening them in Luanda, feeding them well and giving them palm oil for their skin. The sick enslaved Africans were isolated from the healthy and were quarantined."[69] The main concern of the Portuguese owners of enslaved Africans was to ensure that these human commodities arrived to foreign markets in good condition. For this reason, they did not give the captives heavy work that could cause any danger to their health while in Africa, but small chores such as as agricultural activities to help sustain the holding camp's food supply.

The waiting period depended on many factors. In general the frequency of return of ships was slow from across the sea. But some records show that there were cases in which enslaved Africans were dumped in the coastal camps because they were not in good condition or because they were considered beyond the age limit to cross the Atlantic Ocean and do the physical work for which they were enslaved.

Taking into account the total time that enslaved Africans were together (usually six or eight months, sometimes one or two years) before being selected by the merchants and shipped, it can be assumed that the time period was favorable for taking stock of a culture among enslaved Africans. In spite of separate quotas, enslaved Africans purchased in the African market had time to participate in a new lifestyle using the cultural inventory between them. In other words, because enslaved Africans came from the same African market, there was a great possibility that they had certain elements in common. To sum up, "Each group has a history. The people and events can be distinguished. But what calls our attention is that in memory the similarities emerge in the foreground."[70] These "similarities" are what we call common cultural denominators; they find their vital basis not in the origin and nature of individual structure of memory, but under the conditions shared jointly by a new group. In the words of Halbwachs, they constitute "the collective frames of memory" derived from "the social frames of memory."

"The collective frames of memory," Halbwachs tells us, "are precisely the instruments which the collective memory uses to recompose the image of the past that contains, in each time, the dominant thoughts of the society."[71] But these instruments rest on a combination of three main factors for their existence, which were extracted from the society in general, or from many groups. They are (1) the language used to distinguish between objects, people, places; (2) homogeneous time and space, such as those made by collective experience; and (3) a world and logic of experience, such as that established and developed by the group.

Reconsidering the conditions under which the quotas for enslaved Africans from the Kongo were filled, these requirements may be included among the major features of their collective memories. On one hand, the linguistic unification is due to the fact that the majority of enslaved Africans were caught in the Kingdom of Kongo or in neighboring coastal regions (the land of Mbundu) with almost the same linguistic affinities. On the other hand, the time that enslaved Africans spent together was enough for them to homogenize a world of experiences that affected their consciousness and their notion of space. To rebuild this experience, according to Halbwachs, "We need the notion of this medium to be present in it, so that this moment can be represented in it..."[72] But, as we have already mentioned above, the concept of the medium is retained in the essence of three vital factors for the creation of "collective frames of memory."

While crossing the Atlantic, the ships were sometimes forced to stop in other slave markets to complete the loading. The island of São Tomé, where enslaved Africans from both Sudanic and Bantu Africa were found, was often used for this purpose. In this way, it would not be wrong to think that on these occasions, there was a chance that enslaved Africans—not only of different groups but also with different collective memories—mixed, and a new collective memory formed during their shared coastal waiting period.

The nature of the treatment they received on the ship during the trip's 35 to 60 days was characterized by the lack of any activity similar to that allowed on the coast. In other words, the trips were characterized by difficult periods during which a new collective memory germinated. But at the same time, there were periods during which the development of the crystallized collective memories was assured by their individual memories, using its "social framework of memory"—the presence of others with whom they shared the event. There was an intentional displacement of enslaved Africans in the slave markets in Brazil, which did not prevent the sale of these enslaved Africans within the same region in Brazil. This explains the regional concentration of enslaved Africans coming from a certain region of Africa (e.g., Congo, Angola, and Senegambia). Their large numbers assured the continuity of their cultural elements as it was retained in the collective memories of different quotas. According to statistics extracted from municipal records for the sale of enslaved Africans between 1838 and 1860, Carlos Ott reveals that the number of Bantu people was much lower than the Sudanese, who were led by the Nagô (Yorùbá) group.

In the history of Brazilian slavery, a great number of enslaved Bantu peoples (Angola and Congo) were sold legally and illegally in Rio de Janeiro and in the neighboring regions.[73] After the abandonment of agricultural activities in favor of more productive activities such as mining in Mato Grosso and Minas Gerais, many enslaved Africans were released, sold to other owners, or migrated along with their owners. Sociologists, anthropologists, and economists have discussed this aspect of internal migration of enslaved Africans extensively, each stressing their own point of view. Roberto C. Simonsen assigns the massive migration to the south as a search for economic resources. These migrations reflect the Bantu, whose presence in the northern states was recorded since the beginning of the seventeenth century during the Dutch occupation in Angola and Pernambuco for more than a decade. The participation of the Bantu or of their slaveholders in the sugar industry, tobacco culture, gold mining, and cultivation of cotton, rice, or coffee determined their internal migrations, leading to their regional concentration after emancipation.

According to Simonsen, "The fertile lands in the Northeast Brazil and the development of sugar trade resulted in the construction of mills and the planting of sugarcane to a large extent. These industries and cultures later spread to the current state of Rio de Janeiro near the mouth of the Paraíba River."[74] The enslaved Africans were brought to these sugarcane plantations in great numbers to reduce the deficiency of human resources because the indigenous people could not be used in this type of work. There is no written record of the exact number of Bantu peoples in the mills from which sugar production achieved its apogee in the seventeenth century. This production made Brazil the leading producer of sugar in the international market. The Bantu were the first Africans imported by the state of Bahia on a large scale. This high number is confirmed by the strong mark that they left in the culture, language, and folklore of the region, and by the number of merchant ships that anchored in one day in the main port.

Around the end of the seventeenth century, the discovery of gold coincided with the massive drop in the price of sugar. The British Caribbean, the French, and the Dutch had long been prospecting for gold. Simonsen concludes that due to the lure of gold and the economic depression in sugarcane areas, there was a massive migration from milling regions and other locations in Brazil towards the mining lands (see Map IV). The development of gold mining, and other industries that followed, promoted even more enslaved importation from Africa. This changed the points of landing to the nearest ports, such as Parati (Rio de Janeiro) and the bays around Ubatuba, on the north coast of São Paulo. Over the years, these were the ports through which the largest part of illegal transatlantic slaving was conducted. Writing about this subject, Pierre Verger concluded, "During this period (1851), the traffic was concentrated in Rio de Janeiro, Angola, and Congo, according to the commercial habits established at the time of the legal trade."[75] Virgílio Noya Pinto reports that the majority of enslaved Africans came from other parts of Brazil to Minas Gerais, and that they were brought due to the discovery of gold and diamonds in the region. According to Noya Pinto, from a cultural point of view, more important is the fact that the living conditions in the mines were very different from that of the agricultural regions. In the agricultural regions, the enslaved African enjoyed a certain freedom after planting while waiting for the harvest period. During this period, enslaved Africans could do many things of their own choosing. But in the mines, enslaved Africans had to work all the time and the only time given to them for rest was the religious holiday, during which they had to take part in processions with the rest of the brotherhood.

Map IV: The main domestic migrations in Brazil from 1560 to 1940: gold exploration and diamonds in Mato Grosso, Goiás and Minas Gerais, 1700-1760. Reproduced from Roberto C. Simonsen, "Recursos Econômicos e Movimento de Populações."

Noya Pinto later pointed out one of the important reasons that justified the concentration of large numbers of enslaved Africans in the mining areas. He revealed that the lifespan of an enslaved African in an agricultural region was fifteen years, while in the mines it was only seven years. Therefore, to meet the great labor demands in the mines, a great number of enslaved Africans were continuously supplied at a high price, not only from other parts of Brazil but also from the slave markets for Africans (especially Angola and Kongo) to Rio de Janeiro.

The presence of Africans in the mining areas of Mato Grosso is supported by the existence of isolated communities of Africans in this state and whose cultures, passed from one generation to the next, are still similar to that of African cultures. In Minas Gerais, there are small scattered communities found in the south of the state, such as Divisa Nova and São Brás of Suaçul, who practice to this day the traditions of their Bantu ancestors such as the designation of children, the rituals of marriage, etc.

In the middle of the eighteenth century, the majority of the first interior cities built in the area surrounding the mines started to experience some difficulty in feeding their growing populations due to the agriculturally worthless land. Among other things, this was the reason that some owners of less productive mines sold their stakes and changed to a new economic activity such as coffee cultivation, which was being initiated in Vale do Paraíba in the states of Rio de Janeiro and São Paulo around 1810. People from the north, where the tropical crops were stagnant, also moved to these areas.

The last migratory phase, and the one which is of interest, was promoted by the discovery of suitable land for the cultivation of coffee in the west of São Paulo state around the last quarter of the nineteenth century. The effect of the subsequent demographic decline in Vale do Paraíba was also felt in Rio de Janeiro, where many ports that were used for the export of agricultural products and minerals had to be abandoned because of the lack of activity, now shifted to Santos. Consequently, many slaveholders moved with their enslaved Africans to the new lands; others resigned and sold their enslaved Africans to the south, where there was still great demand for their work, or released enslaved Africans on the eve of general emancipation of enslaved Africans in 1888.[76]

After the emancipation, many formerly enslaved Africans preferred to stay around the abandoned mines, particularly in the south of Minas Gerais, the coffee plantations in Vale do Paraíba and in Rio de Janeiro (in the Fluminense region), where they lived in small, isolated communities, showing resistance to white influence for a considerable period of time. Aparecida, one of the smallest cities in Vale do Paraíba appears to be of great importance especially from the cultural point of view. On October 12, 1974, I visited the area on the 257th anniversary of the appearance of the image of Nossa Senhora Aparecida. There, besides the music and the dance style presented by Congada de São Benedito and the group Moçambique in Guaratinguetá, I was particularly amazed with the physical similarity of blacks, who came from neighboring towns to participate in the commemoration on this occasion, with the members of the societies Bakongo and Bazombo from Congo. A curious fact of Bantu concentration in the Vale do Paraíba was observed in the marketplace. There, an old black woman smoked one cigarette with the lit side in her mouth. This practice, common among the women of those societies of Congo, prevailed until the years of independence. Mr. Geraldino de Freitas, an old black man born in April 29, 1901, says with pride that he was 3rd Sergeant from Reserva do Exército, the 10th infantry of Juiz de Fora, who had migrated to Aparecida in 1911. He not only remembers with certainty the Bantu origin of his parents, but when asked about the smoking style with the fire inside the mouth, Mr. Geraldino replied, "My mother also used to smoke like this." Similar practices were noticed in the 1920s by professor Orlando Bastos among the blacks of Divisa Nova (south of Minas Gerais) and I recently had the opportunity to see this in the Fluminense area of Rio de Janeiro.

A recent statistical survey, in the state archives of São Paulo, was done on the census in all cities that make up Vale do Paraíba during the nineteenth century and it confirms the great migration of blacks from the northern states (particularly Bahia and Pernambuco) to the region. It is appropriate to note here that, in this period, not all "blacks" were enslaved Africans; records show that some of them were already free. It also notes that, in addition to their origin here in Brazil, there were also terms such as *crioulo*, *Congo*, and *Kansanje* to designate the ones born in Brazil and the newcomers from Kongo and Kasanje (in the Angola region), respectively.

On the basis of these discoveries, it would not be too bold to say that the Bantu culture, introduced in Vale do Paraíba during the coffee cultivation era, prevailed over its Sudanese counterpart. According Verger, "The Angolans or the Congos as well as the Mozambican are very few in the Bahia state but they comprised the greatest number of enslaved Africans in Rio de Janeiro."[77] What is important to stress here is the fact that Verger, or his source, Castelnau, did not explain the reason for the concentration of the Bantu in Rio de Janeiro, which was already evident in the nineteenth century. Nonetheless, there is little doubt about the Bantu cultural group, their migration to and within

Brazil, and the evolution of its composite culture within the units of Brazilian life, especially the latter's musical elements.

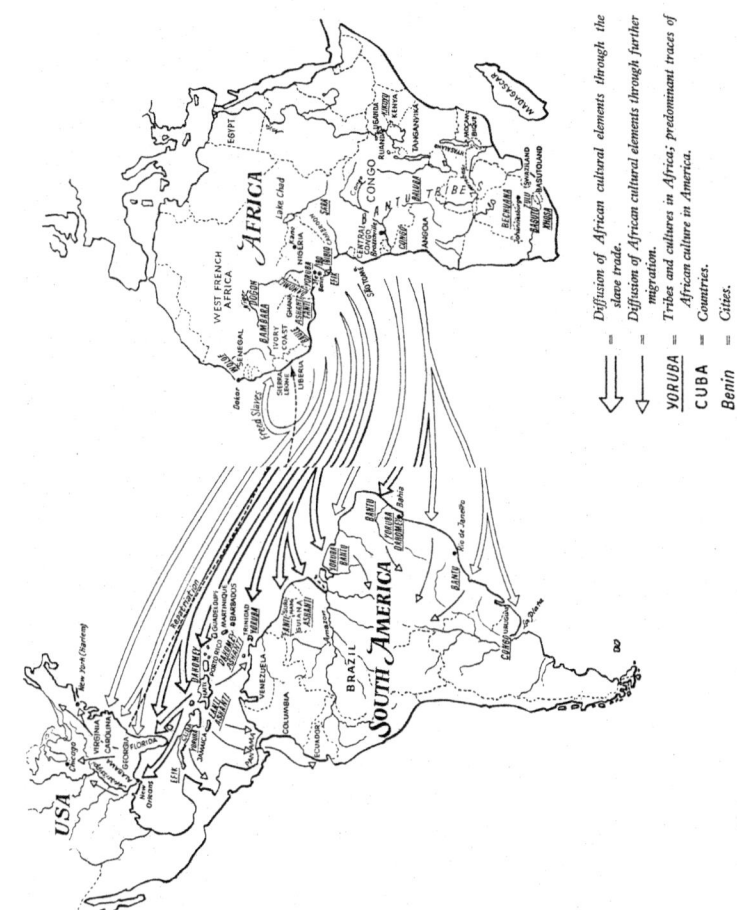

Map VI: Extension of the African culture and the centers of the neo-African culture. Reproduced from Janheinz Jahn, Muntu: Las culturas Neo-African (1963), pp. 24–5.

PART II
IDENTIFICATION AND DETERMINATION

CHAPTER 2

IDENTIFICATION OF BANTU MUSICAL ELEMENTS

For generations, Latin Americanists made generalizations about the spread of African cultural elements to various parts of the Americas. This has introduced errors regarding the footprints left by the enslaved Africans and their descendants in Latin America culture in general, and Brazil in particular. The literature that is currently being published on African culture in the Americas seems to be full of studies that boast these elements but do not attempt to determine or identify its specific African origins. The greater part of this material, written in the first half of the twentieth century, is just an attempt to symbolize the ideology of awakening or "awareness" which was generated during this period by African Americans in search of their identity. This "awareness" has its roots in a concept of retaliatory "blackness," and since then it has had repercussions in the rest of the world, wherever Africans live. In Brazil, this is attributed to the African origins, especially to Bantu and Sudanese origins. The similarities in their basic cultural practices are distinguished by the differences in the philosophy that governs the cultural standards and values and affect the cultural lifestyle.

Sometimes one can find continuities in Brazilians of African descent. These continuities are filled with false information, which claimed that the roots of certain Brazilian cultural expressions may not go back to Africa. In 1941, Melville J. Herskovits published *The Myth of the Negro Past*, and in it he showed the study of "Africanisms," or African survivals, could illustrate cultural continuity between Africa and the Americas. This concern awakened the curiosity of scholars, and was followed in 1967 by Roger Bastide's *Les Amériques Noires*, in which he insisted on the differentiation of the various practices resulting from the operation of various "causalities." Bastide proposed three types of civilizations that should be considered in the study of African diaspora culture in the Americas: they were (a) "Black," the result of pressure from the new environment; (b) "African," the result of an inheritance; (c) "African American," the result of convergence of two similar legacies that merged into one another.

From the definition of these civilizations as given by Bastide, it becomes implicitly evident that the categories can be reduced to one by the merger of two similar inheritances. These were conditioned by the pressure generated by the set of factors present in the new environment. In other words, the three categories fail to consider the context in which each civilization is designed and suggest unlimited and misleading generalizations. If a modification is allowed, we can reduce these categories to two—"African" and "African-Brazilian." The former contains pure legacies (if this is the case) and its variants resulting from processes of acculturation in the new environment. The latter contains African traces but has taken its roots in Brazil.

By removing the word *civilization* from Bastide's categorizations and replacing it with *culture*, there emerges a methodological framework for the detection of Bantu musical elements. This framework borrows its guidelines and structural style from Nina Rodrigues, who was aptly paraphrased by Bastide: "The best method for the analysis of Afro-American [Brazilian] culture is not to study Africa to see what remains of it in America, but to study the existing Afro-American [Brazilian] cultures, to reassemble them progressively to Africa."[78] Taking into account the methodological guideline proposed by Nina Rodrigues, it is the identification of musical elements present in Brazilian musical expression (valuing the cultural background of the forms in which they appear), whose origin can be traced to the Bantu cultural family that is the concern this chapter. Specifically, the chapter is devoted to determining the origins of cultural musical elements identified between the Bantu in Congo and in the Congo-Angola region of cultural interaction.

The presence of Africans and their descendants for almost five centuries in Brazil makes them a valuable cultural constituent whose cultural imprint persisted in many facets of artistic expression. In music, African cultural elements, together with elements of indigenous and European sources, provided a fertile ground for the growth of various religious and secular forms.

These grounds served as a topic for numerous studies in past decades, both by musicologists and folklorists. As is the case with musical syncretism, which results from the meeting of African and European elements, there are African rhythmic concepts of organization. This provides a backdrop against which the European influences, manifested in harmonic and melodic dimensions, are supported.

Little in Brazilian popular music can be claimed as being of Bantu origin due to the considerable amount of similarities in the basic concepts of musical cultures among different African cultural groups. What is believed to be characteristic of a given society is also commonplace in another society of a different cultural family. We must consider several relevant factors in order to determine if this is truly the case—the possible direct or indirect cultural contacts that could have resulted in cultural dissemination between two or more societies. In this case, the criterion of possession of a cultural trait will be assigned to the society in which it will hold a privileged position in any event, regardless of its category (e.g., children's songs, hunting songs, songs of initiation, etc.), because it is not possible to determine the direction in which the influence spread. In Brazilian popular music, the criterion of detection becomes even more difficult due to the evolution of the African musical traits between the time of its inception and the time of its research. A thorough review of its rudiments, however, has revealed its confinement to rhythmic organization.

Pierre Verger assisted on several occasions during a research trip to Salvador (Bahia) in August 1975. He introduced me to Waldeloir Rego, the head of the Department of Culture and Folklore in Salvador. He was the author of the book *Capoeira Angola: Ensaio Sócio-Etnográfico* (1968) and a member of Candomblé de Angola religious center, where he recorded some sessions. On this occasion, he played one of the tapes for us. I recognized the rhythmic standards, implemented in *agogô*, as being of Bantu origin. I asked the pattern names and the response was Kabula and Congo, respectively:

Each one of them emphasizes a rhythmic cloth:

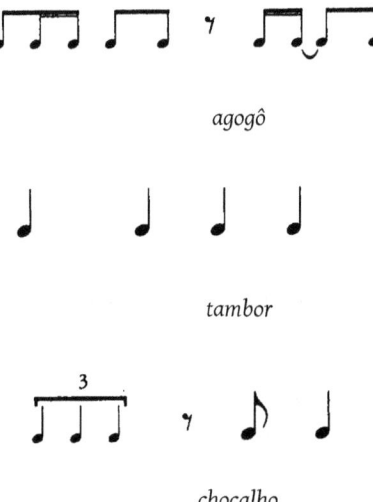

agogô

tambor

chocalho

Some days later, we had a session of Candomble Ketu together with colleagues from Nigeria and the United States. In a tribute to our presence from Congo and Nigeria, the Candomblé priest asked the musicians to perform the rhythmic patterns of Congo and Yorùbá, along with songs in their respective languages. Each one of the visitors was able to recognize a basic rhythmic pattern of his country, and without hesitation we entered in between and performed some dance steps that we used in our countries. It is interesting to note here that the Congo rhythmic pattern, performed also in *agogô*, was identical to the one described above. It provided a "backbone" to the rhythmic improvisations but was also called "Congo," which I did not recognize. What surprised me is that they said my dance was not very different from that of Angola.

Until now, the *samba* (both its music and the dance) has not been adequately studied from a scientific point of view, so the characteristic traits of its rudiments have not been developed. The little that can be found on the subject is scattered in the published reports, mentioned in passing, and mainly boasting of its historical presence and its instrumentation with respect to the *samba* school and the carnival spectacle, or briefly mentioned in folklore studies, or in anthropological studies based on the social ascension of their "black" creators.[79] The historical reports summarized in this study have the sole purpose of providing a cultural background from which the musical analysis will extract its meaning. Although we do not intend to resolve the controversial discussion between Brazilian historians and curious lay readers, our work elucidates this discussion with new and valuable insights that are often ignored.

The idea that the word *samba* is derived from the Bantu word *semba* (Angola, to the precise) is still hypothetical, although Edison Carneiro, quoting Mata Machado Filho, says that this word—*semba*—remains in the mining area where, still today, the African-Brazilians will correct someone who says *samba* with the word *semba*.[80] Field research was carried out in several mining regions in 1975 and this term, however, was not found in use. On the other hand, upon examination of earlier writings by individuals such as Alfred de Sarmento, Capelo, Ladislau Batalha, and Major Dias de Carvalho, who visited the Congo-Angola area in the last quarter of the nineteenth century, the word *semba* was only used in this area to designate the same dance for which the term is used in Brazil.

The use of the word *batuque* (probably Portuguese, meaning *beat*) could be attributed to the linguistic ignorance of some earlier writers, who preferred to use the word to designate the same type of dance that is known in Brazil as the "dance of *umbigada*," considered a precursor to the current *samba*. According to Alfred de Sarmento, who observed the "dance of *umbigada*" in region of Luanda, "The *batuque* consists...of a circle formed by dancers; a black man or a black woman goes to the middle who, after performing several steps, gives an umbigada, also called semba, to the person whom he or she chooses, who then goes to the middle of the circle to replace him/her."[81] For the region of Caconda,

Capelo and Ivens write about *batuque*: "From two groups, individuals leave alternately in the ample space and show their choreographic knowledge, having grotesque attitudes. In general, these are represented by erotic mimicry that the ladies strive to make obscene...after three or four laps around the spectators, the dancer ends by giving his own belly to the first *nymph* who appears, and she repeats the identical scene."[82] "Among the gentle Kongo," writes Carneiro, "the *batuque* is a kind of pantomime in which the subject is always the story of a virgin to whom the mysterious pleasures that wait her are explained, when the *lembramento* [*alambamento* is an indigenous type of marriage] changes her status, are clear evidence of depravity that exists among the inhabitants of hinterland."[83] This observation among the Kongo could be explained by the fact that the dance described above is performed during the initiation of girls, and that the pantomime is commonly sung by mature members. In the upper Congo, the entire ceremony is known as *kikumbi* and this type of song is sung to the suitor (see Example 1). It should also be noted that this initiation is not for puberty, but it precedes marriage and the main subject is sexual education.

Based on these published descriptions, the choreography of *umbigada* resembles that of a circular dance.[84] It was known to several societies (*mbenga* and *lutuku*, among the Luba) around the Congo Basin and always performed by a mixed group in the moonlight. At the end of the century in Kinshasa, *abgaya* came to be known as the precursor of Congo's modern music. Gardel provides a description of *umbigada*:

> The performers stand in circle, singing and rhythmically clapping while one or more persons dance in the middle. They stir their legs, their hips, and their arms with great agility, in synchrony with the drums and other percussion instruments. At some point, the person in the middle chooses one of the people in the circle to occupy his/her place in the middle and makes a sign in the form of a slight touch...Originally, this touch was near the navel, but later used as more subtle invitation. The dancer gave a slight touch to his/her right foot or

foot of the chosen person, who then goes inside the circle to display his/her ability as a dancer.[85]

Mwaku waku nani

Example 1
"Mwaku waku Nani"
(Oral Tradition. Transcribed by the author.)

According to Paulinho da Viola, interviewed on July 20, 1975, the touching of the foot was a test of strength among the dancers. Equally important was the fact that the dance displayed by people in the middle of the circle had a specific character: the doubling of the basic counterpoint rhythmic pattern with the sound of step. This practice, which was also present in *mbenga* among the Luba, came to be an important trait of the old *samba*. It was known by the name of *samba de umbigada*, and by the same fact, it became the characteristic trait of the variants of *samba* in Brazil. In his study, *Samba de Umbigada* (1961), Edison Carneiro created a table of these variants of *samba* (cf. Table I).

TYPES OF SAMBA IN BRAZIL, PAST AND PRESENT

Variants	Belly button	Type of dance
Lundu	X	DBB
Baiano	X	CD
Maranhão		
Tambor de Crioula	X	DBB (l)
Rio Grande do Norte		
Bambelo	X	DBB
Ceara – Paraíba		
Coco	–	CD
Piauí	X	DBB
Milindo	–	CD
Pernambuco		
Coco de troca de parelhas	–	CD
Coco de cordão	–	LD
Coco de roda	X	DBB
Coco de pares	X	CD
Coco mineiro-pau	–	CD

Alagoas		
Coco de visita	X	CD
Coco solto	X	CD
Coco virado	X	DBB
Coco de parelha	-	CD-DC
Coco em fileira	-	LD
Bahia		
Samba de roda	X	DBB
Bate-paú	X	CD
Guanabara		
Partido alto	X	DBB
São Paulo		
Samba de roda	-	DC
Samba rural	-	LD
Samba-lenço	X	LD-CD
Batuque	X	LD
State of Rio de Janeiro (Paraíba Valley)		
Jongo	X	CD

Legend: LD—Line Dance; CD—Couples Dance; DC—Dance in Circle; DBB—Dance of the Belly Button

This table is slightly modified. The term Samba is omitted in the repetition in Ceara-Paraíba, Pernambuco, Guanabara and São Paulo, for being a regional variant of the same genre – Samba. Terms such as "Batuque" and "Jongo" are indicated in certain areas as their presence is the same. This table is reproduced from Edison Carneiro, Samba de Umbigada (1961: 33).

An examination of the works published on *samba* by Brazilian scholars reveal that the enigma of "when and where," which led to this form of popular musical expression and internationally acclaimed as the representative of Brazilian popular music, has called more attention to *samba* than did the probable evolutionary origin or the means by which it could have arisen. According to Carneiro, the *samba de roda* of Bahia was brought to Rio de Janeiro by effluxes of Bahian people who migrated from Canudos. This rhythm announced its arrival to the urban music of *lundu* and *modinha*, and gave birth to a fusion along with the *ranchos de reis* and the *samba* schools, without losing their individuality.

This view, shared by Donga (one of the *samba* pioneers of Rio de Janeiro), also influenced Gardel. In an interview published in a 1965 edition of the *Correio da Manhã* of Rio de Janeiro, Donga said that the *samba* was born in the state of Bahia where it developed in ranches, from where it came to the city street. In his judicious research on the subject, Gardel says, "The approximate date of introduction of the *samba* in Rio de Janeiro has been fixed sometime around the turn of the century."[86] Economic discoveries since the sixteenth century led to migratory movements that resulted in the concentration of emancipated enslaved Africans, mainly of Bantu origin where the tangible evidence is still persistent in culture of the Paraíba Valley. Taking this into account, one may partially agree with Tinhorão, though he does not specify a date but rather says that the *samba* was not introduced in Rio de Janeiro from any other place.[87] He argues the term *samba* was coined in the area of Saúde, where the first carnival dancing appeared around 1870. According to Tinhorão, the birth of *samba* must be placed within the period of sixty years that coincides with the decline of the tobacco crop and cotton in Bahia and with the cultivation of coffee in the Paraíba Valley, between 1870 and 1930.

This view, which we share with Tinhorão, can still be examined further to reveal the logic it possesses. On one hand, the fact that the *samba* is often associated with the Bahians, who attended the Praça Onze in Rio de Janeiro during the turn of the century, does not mean that they migrated with the musical form of their home region. Logically speaking, it is possible that the rhythmic elements of *samba* could have been inherited from songs such as the *lundu* or *modinha*, which were popular in Bahia. During the seventeenth century, it reached the new agricultural centers such as the Valley of Paraíba with enslaved Africans coming from the north, where their slaveholders had left their unprofitable activities for new and lucrative coffee farms. If the first and last migrants from the north (in Bahia) to the coffee area (Vale do Paraíba) already knew about these two forms, one can safely say that the latter is an expression that emerged from the new environment: an environment that received newcomers from Africa (in the Congo-Angola area), with the practice of *lundu* and the dance of *umbigada*. Those two forms were already popular in Portugal by the end of the seventeenth century due to the Brazilian Caldas Barbosa (1738–1800) and could also be considered as precursors of modern *samba*.

In an eighteenth century manuscript on *modinha* found by Béhague in Biblioteca da Ajuda (Lisbon), an anonymous composer clearly indicates that "this accompaniment must [have been] touched by Bahia." Béhague noted that the follow-up that the composer was referring to is dominated by the following rhythmic motif:

Probably a variant of the following:

Lundu, a form of song and dance of African origin (i.e., the Congo-Angola area), was also popular during the seventeenth century in Brazil and Portugal. According to Oneyda Alvarenga, the movements are similar to those of the *batuque* or *samba* de umbigada. Alvarenga notes, "In the center of a circle of spectators, a soloist pair develops the dance which consists of tap-dance. As an urban dance, it had some civilized polishing that transformed the rough primitive sensuality of the batuque to voluptuous, sensual and swing."[88] Lundu is practiced today in region of Franca (São Paulo) which is the only place where this form is still practiced, although it is in danger of extinction. This observation by Alvarenga is true for the *modinha* that became the music of ballroom dance and that adopted a new character in the nineteenth century—a character strongly marked by rhythm of the waltz and influenced by the Scottish. According to Behague, the melodic line *modinha* suffered during the nineteenth century was a transformation by the constant use of ornamentation.[89]

In the rhythmic realm, it could be postulated that *modinha* should have been influenced by *lundu*, which is characterized until today by the systematization of syncope with the same basic reason:

But this syncope is materialized in *lundu* by use of ligature over the bar as follows:

We see this in vocal line, a practice that began to characterize the *samba* since the nineteenth century.

While its musical character is mainly rhythm-based, the *samba* seems to have inherited its organization from *lundu* instrumental traits. According to Candle, it is similar to that of the game and the dance of *umbigada* based mainly on percussion, but in opposition to the stringed instruments (viola and guitar) that constitute the set of monitoring of *lundu* (or *modinha*).[90]

Regardless of what may be the exact date on which this form of popular expression had been created, we can certainly say that the *samba* was already in vogue around November 15, 1878 when it first appeared in the *Gazeta de Notícias* of Rio de Janeiro, in the announcement of the pantomime, *Aladdin and the Magic Lamp*, in which people were invited to take part in "the Samba"—the most authentic success of the season, genuinely fun and popular.[91] That date was ten years before the abolition of slavery in Brazil and seven years after Law No. 2040 of September 28, 1871 declared free status for the children of enslaved African women born since that date and freed enslaved Africans of the state. Our argument about the date of creation of *samba* is a fact that confirms the narrow time period of only eight years, from 1870 to 1878, suggested by Tinhorão. On the other hand, this period coincides with the decline of the coffee culture in the Paraíba Valley and the discovery of suitable land for agriculture in a plateau of western São Paulo, which forced an influx of migrants from the north to this area. Hence, it would not be wrong to argue that the *samba* was not introduced but evolved in the new community, and most probably in one of the cities of the Paraíba Valley where the coffee culture was the main source of economic exploitation. In spite of this, why not the Fluminense region (Rio Janeiro), where, at the time, it spread finally to the entire nation?

In the beginning, the *samba* was not accepted easily by the so-called "fine-grain" or "conventional" sectors of society. Its social rise, parallel to their black creators, found severe restrictions from the authorities, which associated *samba* with gang fights and other disturbances. Several reports from some of the pioneering figures of *samba*, in Rio de Janeiro, are given by João Baptista Borges Pereira, in his book *Cor, profissão e mobilidade* (1967). In the following statements, the difficulties encountered by *samba* and its creators are revealed in two personal accounts:

An 87 years old man of mixed heritage related these memories:

> My mother always had parties to gather my friends and colleagues of black origin. The feast lasted sometimes for days. There were refreshments in the ballroom, the striped *samba* (loud party) in the back room and drumming in the yard. To give the party, my mother would seek a permit from the police, as people thought the blacks came together only to fight or to do trickery. Even with permission, the police did not let the people be in peace. She hated them always. When the police 'pressed' everyone in a corner, we went to another. We did plain *samba*. When the police came, we hid on the hill. Before inhabiting the hills, people already had *samba* there. The hill was the only hiding place for the city *sambista*, from the plain. One day in May of 1918, I was on the rock, attending the party and *samba*. The police always took our instruments because they thought that black was quarrelsome, and that the *capoeira* and percussion instrument served as a weapon.[92]

A 67 years old black person also recalled:

> When I was a little boy, I would watch the *samba* of blacks out in the woods, near the mangroves. They chose the place where the police could not find them. I remember once I was watching quietly when the police came. They broke the instruments and made the blacks run. When I grew up, by 1920, the people walked with hidden instruments when they went from one feast to another. Whenever anyone put a guitar under his arm, the police came. *Samba* was the name that made the higher class make the sign of the cross. But all of these have passed and today I, who once ran from the police, am honored by all…our music was a cause of shame, today it is our pride.[93]

In 1917, while the *sambistas* were still running from the police and the *samba* struggled to be accepted in the halls, the first recording of a song—"By Phone"—officially recognized as *samba* was produced in Rio de Janeiro. This music, jointly written by the companions of feasts and serenades who attended the house of Aunt Ciata in Square 11, is today often attributed to Donga, a member of the group, who recorded on his own. But some of the eyewitnesses of the period still protest against this assignment. Pereira records the testimony of a 77-year old black man, who recalled, "There were many houses where the blacks met. The main, that I remember, was of Perciliana, mother of João da Baiana; Amélia of Aragão, mother of Donga; and aunt Ciata in Square 11, where *samba* 'By Phone' was recorded but Donga says that it belonged to him."[94]

In spite of the persecutions of the *samba* and its creators, it became popular in the country during the early 1900s, acquiring characteristics and names that varied with local-regional styles (cf. Table I). The variants of *samba* can certainly be divided into two main categories, distinguishing the "rural" and "urban" forms. Observation and personal participation in *samba* of both categories have revealed a slight difference, especially in the choreographic interpretation, while musically they remain basically the same. Of the two categories, the urban, especially in Rio de Janeiro, is subject to constant change, due to the continuous foreign influences to which it is exposed. In 1962, the assimilation of foreign traits by *samba* had become a huge concern. Under the sponsorship of the Confederação Brasileira das Escolas de Samba (CBES), the Associação Brasileira das Escolas de Samba (ABES), the Campanha de Defesa do Folclore Brasileiro, the Conselho Nacional de Cultura, and the Ordem dos Músicos do Brasil met at the Palácio Pedro Ernesto in Rio de Janeiro. Their main interest was to elaborate the first *carta do samba* and met under the presidency of Edison Carneiro, the during the first Congresso Nacional do Samba, between November 28 and December 2. The purpose of the letter, as mentioned in its written introduction by the elected president, was to establish a series of recommendations aimed at protecting and preserving the characteristics of *samba*. A passage from the introduction reads, "The Samba Congress...accept[s] the normal evolution of *samba* as an expression of the popular joys and sorrows; we want to create conditions by which this evolution takes place naturally as a real reflection of our life and of our customs; but we also recognize the dangers that surround this evolution, trying to find ways and means to neutralize them."[95] The *sambistas*, as determined by the letter, should remain aware of fundamental rhythms of traditional *samba*; in adaptation, they should ensure that other genres were adapted to *samba* and not the reverse.

An examination of the forms of *samba*, in rural or urban areas, reveals the predominance of a basic rhythmic pattern used both in melodic organization and in accompaniment. Symbolically, it and its variants can be represented as follows:

Comparing these patterns with those discussed in *lundu* and *modinha*, one can hardly deny their similarity. In his musical analysis dedicated to melodic organization of rural *samba* in the interior of São Paulo, Mario de Andrade provides several melodic transcripts that qualify as the basic rhythmic pattern characteristic of *samba* performed by *bombo*:

On other hand, Menezes Bastos, by assigning the same pattern of African origin, stresses that its influence is felt in various musical forms in Brazilian folklore, such as the *fandango*, as described by Mario de Andrade around 1927 in Cananéia (São Paulo) (see Example 2).[96]

CHAPTER 2

Ex. nº 2
Fandango

Example 2
"Fandango"

Equally important for the present study, however, is the as-yet unexplored rhythmic cycle which in the beginning was confined to urban *samba* in its popular form, but today is also found in rural *samba* and other variants, as mentioned in Table I. Here it is:

Sometimes it is heard in the following version:

These two rhythms of *samba*, i.e., the legacy of *lundu* and the cycle, can be considered as the more representative *samba* rhythm, especially in its popular form.

Structurally the rhythmic cycle, often given by the orchestration of tambourine percussion or by *cavaquinho* (small guitar-like instrument) in orchestration with stringed instruments, can be divided into two main segments of seven and nine quavers according to the reference density chosen, divided into the sharp beat cycle. Analytically, it is presented as follows:

In total, sixteen quavers, or when reduced to a reference of lower density, it must contain sixteen semi-quavers in organized binary rhythm. The variation of the cycle, used according to the preference of the artist, is divided and marked by pause until establishing the end of the first segment (motif):

It should be noted here that, during the execution, the pause at the end of the first motif focuses on an even stronger accent in the previous eighth note. For many years, this practice was considered by the German school and by the disciples of Hornbostel to situate the important point in rhythmic organization, as was conceptualized by the Africans in the pause—not in the previous knock as highlighted above.

Functionally, the cycle, with its rhythmic motif (when played in conjunction with a bombo [drum]), serves not only to give a rhythmic cover but also to mark a time line. Kwabena Nketia refers to it as a constant reference point by which the structure of a song phrase as well as the metric linear organization of the sentence is conducted. In *samba* songs, this pattern combines very well with the phrase divisions in melodic lines. For each melodic segment, there is a complete rhythmic cycle (see Examples 2 and 4).

CHAPTER 2

The characteristic function of the cycle can be observed virtually in most Brazilian *sambas* taught by numerous *samba* schools and by joint monitoring of popular musicians. In both cases, the rhythmic cover is composed of two main patterns, notably the following:

Its variants can be combined with

or variants as follows:

In the instrumental resources of Brazilian popular music, there have appeared many cases where it would be risky to label some instruments as being of Bantu origin due to their diffusion throughout Africa and Europe. For some, this diffusion can be certainly traced to a given cultural region regardless of subsequent local-regional modifications, which can be partly attributed to the material available in the culturally uniform environment of their manufacturers. In Brazil, despite being industrialized, the instruments have preserved their organological structure, which makes it easier to track their respective origins. These instruments were diffused widely among African societies, however, and their origin cannot be definitively attributed to the Bantu region (specifically, Congo-Angola). From a cultural point of view, they can be considered the creators of a set of common cultural denominators in the artistic expression of enslaved Africans in the Americas.

One of these instruments is the *campânula dupla* (double bell) of high tones (small) and low (wide) or male and female, stuck on the edges of a bent metal rod. This type of bell is common in Africa and known between the Bakongo of Congo as *ngongi*, or as *nkobu* among the Luba. In Brazil, it adapted the name *Yorùbá de agogô*. Regardless of the religious and popular orchestration in which it appears, the *agogô* fulfills a function varying from one region to another. In some regions, such as among the Luba of Mutumbi, the instrument has the unique function of giving a rhythmic counterpoint motif to the motif given by the same drum set. In other regions such as that occupied by the Akan of Ghana, two or three *agogô* of different shades are sometimes used to create a harmonic and rhythmic supplement to the vocal melody and at the same time to mark the division of time (time line) of the entire composition. For some indigenous healers or spiritualists, the *agogô* was a valuable instrument for their invocations.

In Brazil, with the industrialization of *agogô* aimed at improving sound quality, *samba* schools have specific specimens bearing characteristics of the school. Its functions have not been modified, however; it continues to give basic rhythmic patterns, both in religious assemblies and in popular music.

CHAPTER 2

Tristeza Pé no Chão

Example 3
"Tristeza Pé no Chão"
(From Armando Fernandes's "Mamão" recorded by Clara Nunes—SBRXLD
12353 recording ODEON—1973; transcribed by the author).

Example 4
"Minha Festa"
(From Nelson Cavaquinho and Guilherme de Brito; recorded by Clara Nunes—SBRXLD 12353 recording ODEON—1973; transcribed by the author).

Another widely known instrument in Africa is the rattling of a basket which has survived in Brazil in its minor form, associated with *capoeira* and also used in Candomble (e.g., Angola, Gegê-Nagô, and Caboclo).[97] In Bahia, where this form of choreographic fight is frequently practiced, the rattling basket is known as *caxixi*, a name that has been attributed to its larger size specimen found in Museu de Folclore in Lapa. In Brazil, the origin of the instrument and the name by which it is called were probably unknown in 1968 when Waldeloir Rego published his valuable book, *Capoeira Angola: Ensaio Sócio-Etnográfico*. Rego wrote, "Nothing concrete is known about the origin of the name or the instrument."[98] This opinion, which may have been based solely on Brazilian data without taking into account the African sources, is no longer valid because of recent evidence drawn from African societies. Organologically, Rego described the instrument it in these terms, "The *caxixi* is a small rattle made of woven straw with base gourd (Cucúrbita lagenaria, Linneu), cut into circular shape and the top line, ending with a handle in the same straw... inside the *caxixi*, there are dry seeds which give the characteristic bobbing" sound. One of their characteristic physical features evident in its original form is the gourd piece at the base of the instrument and placed upside-down. In some Brazilian specimens, the gourd is sometimes replaced by a piece of wood.

According to Candeia, this instrument was used in *jongo* together with percussion instruments, fulfilling the same function of the *maracá* or rattling drum in numerous *samba* schools, marking or highlighting the underlying density. In *capoeira*, the *caxixi*, which is used along with the musical bow (*berimbau*), doubles the rhythmic pattern given by the metal rod in the stick of the *berimbau*, and gives rhythmic ornamentation between the basic rhythms marked on the bow.

On other hand, there are the *sanza* and the *marimba*, which are recorded as having been used during the eighteenth and nineteenth centuries in Brazil. A discussion on *sanza* is not included here because the only specimen found was seen in the Museu do Folclore, in Ibirapuera (São Paulo), in a non-functional state. The *marimba*, on the contrary, is still in use in the small community of São Francisco, on the northern coast of São Paulo. Although simplified, the structure of *marimba* still preserves the morphological aspect of Africa. In São Francisco, where Kilza Setti found the instrument in 1972, his informant Casimiro Camilo dos Santos confirmed the antiquity of the specimen, which became very useful during the presentation of the Congada on the day of St. Benedict. According to Casimiro, the instrument was a community property and stored in the home of the "King" of Congada, Sr. Antonio Bernardino Tavares, a white Brazilian who was also the community's political leader. Kilza observed, in an informal conversation, that the player of the instrument during Congada won a certain societal respect for their musical role.

In the set of musical instruments still in use on the Brazilian musical scene, there are two that can be proven with certainty to be of Bantu origin. One of them, the *berimbau*, was introduced in popular music only recently. Since its arrival in the Americas, it has been confined to the musical world of *capoeira*. The other, a friction drum, the *cuíca*, occupies a prominent position, particularly in sets of *samba*.

The term *berimbau*, derived from the Kimbundu term *mberimbau*, has been adapted in Brazil to designate a type of musical bow which is today associated with the game and martial art of *capoeira*. The latter is practiced throughout the country and has its highest concentration in Bahia, Rio de Janeiro, Minas Gerais, and São Paulo. The enigma of its adaptation has yet to be unveiled by ethnographers, anthropologists, linguists, ethnomusicologists, and scholars from other related scientific fields.

In his *Tratado da Terra e da Gente do Brasil*, Fernão Cardim speaks of the Christmas of 1584, in the Colégio dos Jesuítas in Rio de Janeiro, and brother Barnabé with an instrument called *berimbau*, but with no description. Cardim wrote, "We had a Nativity scene in the town where we sometimes had good and proper music, and brother Barnabé rejoiced with his *berimbau*."[99] Despite the lack of information regarding the morphological aspect of the instrument, it is important to point out that the instrument known as *berimbau* in this period should not be confused with the Brazilian musical bow currently known. The *berimbau* here should be what Antonio de Moraes Silva has defined in his *Dicionário de Língua Portuguesa* as a "sound instrument the size of only five to six centimeters, nearly circular with two extended rods and being crossed by a steel blade; the person applies to his mouth, touching it to his teeth and with his finger vibrates the blade, producing a sound that imitates the name of the instrument."[100] In Europe, especially in France, Germany, England, and Portugal, the instrument was already well known before the late sixteenth century. In Portugal, for example, the instrument must have been common at the beginning of the sixteenth century and definitely before 1550.

In Brazil, the term was originally used with a modifier: *berimbau*-debarriga, designating a musical bow that, until the end of the first half of our century, had not acquired its current organological structure. Câmara Cascudo reports other names by which the instrument was known, including, among others, the name *gunga* that, according to Mestre Noronha, reminds one of a *capoeira* song in which the term is evoked:

> *Este gunga é meu*
>
> *Eu não dou a ninguém*
>
> *Eu trouxe da África...*

In his book *Viagens ao Nordeste do Brasil*, Henry Koster mentions a type of *berimbau* which was used both by enslaved and freed Africans, and describes it along with another instrument: "The musical instruments were extremely rude. One of them is a kind of drum, made from a skin of sheep, stretched on a hollow trunk of tree. The other is a large bow with a rope having a half-shell of coconut in the middle, or a small gourd, tied. It is placed against the abdomen and the rope is touched with finger or a piece of wood."[101] The coconut shell or the position of the gourd mentioned by Koster is important in our analysis because it reveals the possible nature of the instrument, as it was introduced in the country, and its inevitable influence suggests that the instrument must have been transformed in the new environment to acquire its present form and ringing technique. On the one hand, the position of the resonator in the middle of the extended rope suggests the division of the rope in equidistant segments producing the same sound. It is precisely for this reason that this position does not allow the instrument to be held in the same way by known *capoeristas*. On the other hand, plucking the string also certifies its rudimentary condition which, during the arrival period, still was not associated with the game of *capoeira*, but with other social events such as the *samba de roda* (dance of *umbigada*). Koster notes, "The free blacks also danced but were limited to ask permission and his party passed before one of their huts. The dances resemble those of African blacks. The circle was closed and the viola player sat in a corner, and began to play simply, accompanied by some favorite songs, repeating the refrain, and often one of the verses was improvised and contained obscene allusions. A man went to the center of the circle and danced some minutes, taking lascivious attitudes, until he chose a woman singing and repeating the same indicement gestures. This fun lasted sometimes until morning."[102]

Currently the *berimbau* has been exclusively associated with *capoeira*, although some popular musicians, such as João Melo and Codo, are trying to incorporate it into the popular orchestration scene (e.g., the songs "Sambou *samba*" and "*Berimbau* é pau" by the same composers). It should be mentioned at this time, however, that the current instrument differs markedly from the specimen mentioned above. According to Mestre Noronha (who goes by the nickname of David Coutinho), and other teachers and scholars, the *berimbau* is made of the following five components. The first is the *biriba*, the wood to make the bow of the *berimbau* due to its characteristic resistance, about which Mestre Noronha insists that "this wood can resist a large blow and can be used as a weapon by the player during a heavy *capoeira* fight." The second is the *cumbuca*, the name given to the resonator, originally made from a half gourd and the latter currently getting replaced by coconut shell particularly for commercial production. Waldeloir Rego describes its position in the instrument as follows: "It is an opening in part that attaches to the stem and the bottom two holes, through which a cord is passed to connect it to the bow of wood and steel wire."[103] The third is the *fio de aço*, an iron rod extended over the bow and divided into two unequal lengths of the resonator rope. The fourth is the *baqueta*, a piece of wood used to strike the iron rod. Preferably, the baqueta is made of rosewood. Finally, there is the *dobrão*, the currency of the time (more often the 40 réis coin), probably due to its size and width, which allow for better control when pressing against or the hitting action on the rod to change the pitch.

Some characteristics of the instrument are often overlooked by scholars in their descriptions, but were highlighted with emphasis by Mestre Noronha. One is the *courão*—two pieces of leather, the size of tip of the bow, attached by nail or glue to prevent the metal rod from cracking the wood, and at the same time contribute to the quality of the timbre of the instrument. Another is the *caro*—a technical term among the *capoeiristas* that designates a rope (of nylon or other non-metallic wire) tied at one end of the rod to make it easier to tie the rod to the wood.

The description of the monitoring instrument, *caxixi*, was given independently, but it is worth mentioning here that the *caxixi* used in *capoeira* has a special feature which should be considered as a relevant trait. The seeds that it contains must be of the brava type of banana. Being more sensitive to hand movements, they jump at the base of the gourd of *caxixi*.

The execution of *berimbau* is done as follows. The musician holds the instrument in the left or right hand in a vertical position with the third and fourth fingers holding the bow while the little finger wraps the rope of the resonator. Between the thumb and the first finger of the same hand, the musician holds the currency that will interact with the rod. This is to shorten the length of the rope and thus raise the tone of instrument or to produce the rattling effect (known as "buzzing"). On the left or right hand, the musician holds the *caxixi* with the second and third fingers tucked in the handle of the instrument while holding the drumstick with the same hand, as if holding a spoon. During execution, the overall timbre of the instrument is modified by the damping actions of the resonator (the open end) on the chest of the player. The *capoeira* group is composed commonly of three *berimbau*, a hand drum, a tambourine, an *agogô*, and a reco-reco (scrapper), with the background music composed by merging several melodic contour patterns and rhythmic time line cycles. In Angolan *capoeira*, the mixture is made up of *jogo de dentro*, *São Bento grande*, and *São Bento pequeno*. The last two lyrics are played on lighter instruments, while the first is assigned to the master instrument or the "center *berimbau*," which plays the role similar to bass drum and accentuates the structural beat of the composition. According to Mestre Noronha, "The marking of the *berimbau* comes from the center that *capoeira* players should follow with their body movements".

The Brazilian friction drum—*cuíca*—has, for a considerable period, spurred controversial hypotheses that are not so much related to the channel by which it reached Brazil, but are related to its origin and primary use in this country.

As for the origin of *cuíca*, we will leave the discussion to the next chapter. But in addition to the commonly known *cuíca* with the inner rod, there existed, in some period, another species of friction drum having the external rod similar to that found in Portugal. According to Ernesto Veiga de Oliveira, this specimen was called *adufe*, the name by which it is known in Portugal. Veiga de Oliveira notes, "The American fricative, in the more general case of inner rod, no doubt seems to be of black African origin, and therefore excludes any hypotheses of common origins with the Portuguese *sarronca* and Brazilian *puita*, i.e. the diffusion of Portuguese or European *sarronca* (the outer rod) in Brazil (except possibly in the case of the *adufe* which seems to be used in certain parts of the country, and which can certainly be of direct European origin and Spanish or Portuguese specifically)."[104] The author, however, does not specify the time during which the instrument was used in Brazil. In the same source, however, Veiga de Oliveira mentions the use of *puita* in Salvador during Christmas, accompanying the singer of the brotherhood in processions. In the state of São Paulo, the same instrument was also used in certain dances of various localities.

It is interesting to note that the instrument, at that time in its rudimentary form, was made of hollow tree trunk, with one end covered by a membrane, probably goat leather, the middle of which was tied to a rod and the other end was left open where the hand is introduced to get the rod. These days, the instrument has become highly industrialized; all materials have been changed but the overall structure is kept intact. The *cuíca* is rarely used in Christmas festivities but became one of the main instruments of popular music sets and *samba* schools.

CHAPTER 3

DETERMINATION OF CULTURAL ORIGINS OF IDENTIFIED BANTU MUSICAL ELEMENTS

Applying the methodology outlined at the beginning of the previous chapter, our present task is to return to the Congo-Angola area, which, in the first chapter, we referred to as a zone of cultural interaction. Our objective is to investigate the place(s) of origin of Bantu musical traits detected in Brazilian popular music and in the African-Brazilian religions. Accumulated through fieldwork, the musical examples included herein were selected from a broad sample extracted from a wide area that extends from the Shaba region through the area south of Congo-Angola border to the current lower Congo. Information and musical data scattered in regions of Angola are also used to confirm our hypothesis of cultural unity among the Bantu societies that occupied the Kingdom of Kongo and the Congo River Basin, or what we call the "Congo-Angola area." In other words, we must eliminate what some scholars have considered as mere coincidence and show the dissemination of some of these elements through cultural contacts.

In music, the Africanists divide the African continent into several "music cultures" or "musical areas," based on non-musical divisions. Among the most accepted theories of division is the one based on language families, as proposed by linguist Joseph Greenberg, who distinguishes eleven major language families.[105] These families have been reduced by ethnomusicologists into just four large groups. In the musical culture of northern Africa, that is, above the Sahara desert, there are strong Arabic traces in the melodic contour, rhythmic and harmonic interpolation, vocal production and musical instruments, intonation, and mode used. These traits left partial traces in the sub-Saharan musical culture, where the Islamic religion was introduced by Muslims. The area that corresponds to the Sudanic belt extends below the Sahara desert, from the Atlantic Ocean to the Red Sea and Indian Ocean. According to Kwabena Nketia, the Sudanic or Sudanese belt constitutes the second zone of intense cultural integration characterized by the presence of a variety of long trumpets, sitar, lyre, harps, and timpani.[106] The first zone of interaction extends from the western Sudan to Chad and the surrounding area, where a variety of instruments of the family of the lute and harp-lute, and certain traits of the style of singing monodic (i.e., one voice) predominate. On the other hand, Bascom and Herskovits proposed seven main areas and an eighth area, occupied by the Batwa peoples, who lack a geographical unit and are spread over several places in Central Africa.

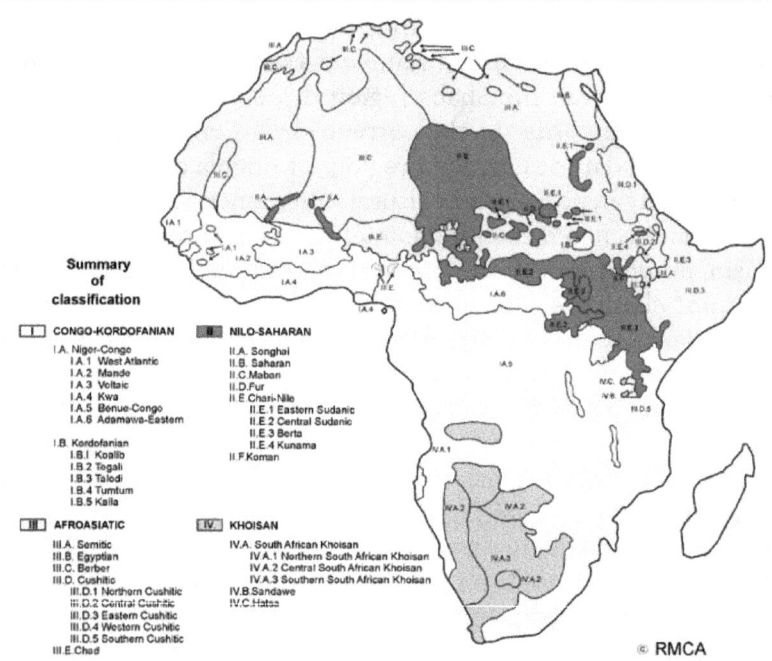

More cultural divisions exists between Bantu and Sudanese musical styles, especially in the geographical distribution of musical instruments and vocal production, both constrained by predominant foreign influence and the geographic space occupied by the cultural groups. In the Bantu in coastal regions, the

Portuguese influence on musical instruments, spanning the late fifteenth to the seventeenth century, is still rooted in the local cultures. For example, the Kikongo word *msaka* ("basket") has a Portuguese origin and is also used to designate a rattle made of cans containing dried seeds. Other foreign influences embedded in traditional musical culture among the Bantu in the Congo-Angola area are manifested in the presence of the accordion, whistle or peawhistle, and military bugle; some even became part of the heritage of some families.

Among the Sudanese people, there are many traits attributed to Islamic musical influences. They are symbolized in the prevalence of the aerophone, known as the *haoussa alghaita*, and the chordophone as the monotone instrument (the *riti* of Wolof musicians in Senegal) belonging to families of double reed musical instruments and the *viela* (violin). Francis Bebey expressed the geographical distribution of this monotone bow violin in these terms: "The stringed friction instrument, best known as monotone alley, was used by musicians from West Africa, particularly in the Islamized regions. It is found, under different names, in the north of Cameroon and Nigeria, in Chad and in almost all the area that runs from the great lake to Senegal. It is the 'riti' of the Wolof of Senegal, the 'nyanyour' of the Toucouleurs, the 'Godie' or 'godji' of Songhais and the Djarmas of Niger..."[107]

A. M. Jones suggests a more specific division based on musical practice. In his *Studies in African Music*, he surveyed the musical traits found among sub-Saharan societies and classified them according to their harmonic practices, i.e., the predominant harmonic interval used by the societies under study. Jones also observed possible subdivisions between societies that occupied the same geographical area, subdivisions that may be determined by characteristic criteria or by identifying features of harmonic style in these musical cultures. Qualifying regions of study according to their predominant harmonic intervals, Jones concluded, "Some societies sing in parallel thirds. The societies who sing this way completely exclude any other range with the exception of some limited cases..." With regard to these limited cases, Jones notes, "There are some societies that live among societies who sing separately (or respectively) in the two traditions (the third tradition and of '8-5-4') and whose harmony was influenced by both. Sometimes, some songs are entirely in parallel thirds and some entirely in the '8-5-4' style, sung by the same societies."[108]

Although these statements should be viewed with some caution due to their rigidity, Jones's effort should not be discredited by suggesting the possibility of diverse musical styles that characterize a musical culture. In rhythmic organization, a similar attempt was made in a more limited area in Congo and organized in a manuscript entitled "Geografia Rítmica da Música Tradicional do Zaire."[109] It had the objective of determining what we call a *símbolo do ritmo* (rhythmic key signature), i.e., the rhythmic patterns characteristic of traditional musical cultures according to the regional divisions in Congo. In other words, each musical culture had some peculiarities in their rudiments (e.g., melodic contour, harmonic and rhythmic organization), musical instruments (organological structure), etc., with which it was identified. Stylistically, the "traits of identity" constitute what is known as the cradle of style in a musical culture, which spread from one region to another, resulting in local-regional variations of the original elements. In time, the local-regional variations acquired sufficient special characteristics to be regarded as a new style. Often, the new style thus obtained is confused with the one from which it was derived, sometimes due to its impressive form in comparison with the latter.

In this case, we are presented with similar situations that remove the cultural boundaries of the regions to which a given form or instrument can be assigned. Keeping in mind the global direction of cultural influences within our area of interest, however, we will postulate that some of the standards included in our list of qualitative contributions of the Bantu in Brazilian popular music did not undergo a modification or variation of original patterns from the interior regions. These were introduced in the coastal regions by migratory groups, who acquired, in some cases, a new feature before being transplanted to Brazil. But this aspect will be discussed later.

On the top of our list, there are the rhythmic patterns of *cabula* and *congo*, each representing its own affinity. An examination of the rhythmic structure of musical sets among Bakongo societies show the predominance of the following rhythmic cycle and its variants:

The majority of these songs are associated with social fun. In the following musical example extracted from the Ntandu repertoire, the cycle is given by *ngongi* on the *agogô* (see Example 5).

Structurally, the similarity between this cycle and that displayed in default *cabula* is undeniable. Yet despite the similarity in structure, there is a relevant difference in the implementation of the component motifs:

In *cabula*, these motifs are executed with equal emphasis on all the notes without a standardized bell, which is the sequence of change in high and low tone of an *agogô*. This is usually left to the discretion of the player who will apply varieties according to his or her degree of virtuosity. Among the Bakongo, the following characteristics are noticeable.

On the one hand, the first motif, when executed in its totality, begins with a jerk in the high tone bell and an accent in each one of the semi-quavers, and the first quavers in the low tone bell to finish with a jerk in the last quaver, playing the bell of high tone. To simplify the reading, this motif can easily be presented as follows:

Note the dots and dashes above the notes to indicate, respectively, the "staccato" (emphasized by a break) and the accent. This is probably the same motif whose pattern was presented by Raul Giovani da Motta Lody in the following version:

This is touched by the *agogô* without any specific tone sequence. The second motif is as follows:

On the contrary, the first two notes (including the notes joined by ligation) are performed in a low bell tone with an accent to close the motif with a "staccato" in a high tone bell. The pause (segment represented in the score by a symbol) in the beginning of the motif suggests a syncope, which is only felt after the accent on the notes joined by ligation. Often, during execution, the high tone beat and the initial beat are omitted, avoiding the repetition of two consecutive beats of a high tone, and by the same fact, marking a slight syncope. Symbolically it looks like this:

Mono Kisala Ko

Ex. n°5

Example 5
"Mono Kisala Ko"
(Kongo oral tradition. Transcribed by the author)

It would not be presumptuous to assign the rhythmic cycle of the *congo* to the area of Bakongo, in which it is predominantly present. However, it should be noted here that, as the majority of cultural practices in the lower Congo, this cycle also has its repercussion among some societies in the northern Angola regions, along the border with Congo. In other words, this region coincides with our imaginary horizontal line referred earlier as the "Congo-Angola" zone of cultural unity.

Contrary to the pattern, the detected cycle of *congo* is widespread throughout Africa.

It occupies a prominent position in most repertoires among the societies of Congo regardless of sex, age, associations, or ceremony (e.g., invocation, mourning). In Shaba, particularly among the Luba-Shankadi, this cycle is an important accompaniment for the majority of children songs sung during the period of initiation, during which they are isolated in a camp outside the village. It also is used in accompanying their competitions within the village. In the first instance, the rhythmic pattern is given by a small drum and beats of the hand; in the latter, the same pattern is confined to the beats of the hand due to a limited number or the absence of accompanying musical instruments.[110]

In the adult musical realm, this cycle is also present in the urban musical form, in the modern "rumba," which has become an identifying element of rhythmic organization.[111] In Central Africa, the pattern that we are presenting here in 4/4 can be divided into ten eighths, taking as reference the density of the eighth note; this was also observed by Jones, who presents it as follows, measured in a 12/8.[112]

Although both rhythmic cycles can be divided into two motifs, it should be noted that, in the cycle presented by Jones, the impression of triplets is not as emphasized as presented in *cabula*. According to Jones's scoring the last note of the first motif indicates the rhythmic disturbance in the beginning of the second motif for each one of these cycles. This practice is intended to create a syncopated impression, while, in our presentation, it is indicated by a pause (segment represented in the score by a symbol) after the triplet components of the first motif.[113]

A predominant rhythmic pattern can be considered an identifying trace of stylistic mode in a musical culture in which it is practiced. The exhaustively discussed cycle, which has the more characteristic pace of *samba*, can be found in many parts of Africa and occupies an important place in some cultures where it assumes a particular form.

In most regions of Africa where it is found, this pattern occurs in conditional or circumstantial occasions and relies greatly on the organization of the poetic text sung, which determines its appropriate sequence of valuing the note. In the following musical transcript from the Hehe peoples of Tanzania, the first motif appears every time the word *kalala* is used:

All the standard appears in relation to the combination of words *kalala kwaku*.[114]

The same principle that governs the structure of a cyclical rhythmic pattern is observed in the following example of a "call and response" song in Makonde society, in northern Mozambique, according to Nketia.[115] Here, everytimethe word *tueje* is used it is sung in the rhythm of the first motif of the cycle.

Makonde Oral Tradition, Northern Mozambique

Example 6
(Makonde oral tradition. Transcribed by Nketia)

Ex. nº 7

These are just two of the many examples found in the various musical cultures of Africa where the linguistic content (including consonants, vowels, nasals, and semi-vowels) is the determining factor, since it reflects the relative duration of the syllables in the rhythmic organization of songs. Nketia explains that this practice is very common among the Akan, the Ga and the Ewe in Ghana, and other various societies in Nigeria.[116] These regions have songs based on the pulse structure equivalent to the first motif, and is often linked to the following syllabic organization summarized in this pattern: *CVV* or *CVN* (that is, Consonant-Vowel-Vowel or Consonsant-Vowel-Nasal consonant).

In some cases, the pattern would not be considered as characteristic of the musical culture, since its chance existence depends on the pace of poetic syllabic organization of a word. It can also be observed that this type of practice, i.e., application of a cycle in a melodic line without considering the linguistic aspect (a practice that does not exist in African languages, but allowed in the majority of European languages), can limit an African singer in any situation of improvisation. In this way, this pattern can hardly be considered in this practice as being stylistic in the rhythmic culture in which it occurs. On the other hand, the same rhythmic cycle forms the basis of the majority of cultural music in the region of Kasai in Zaire (Congo). It is further identified among the Luba as the *Misambu ya Bampamba* and *Misambu ya bipwidi*—music for twins and for social meetings, respectively. Here, in addition to the cases discussed above, the following occupies a prominent position in the overall organization of song; a valid criterion to identify it with the musical culture.

In the joint accompaniment of numerous songs that make up the repertoires of musical categories mentioned above, both identified as activities of singers, the pattern is given by rattles of a basket and gourd, or by *bikashi* (beats of the hand). The following musical examples were chosen from several repertoires of the Luba musical culture of the Kasai region, but an examination of examples of songs from other musical cultures in Congo proves their great confinement to the region from where they must have reached Europe and the Americas, carried by emigrants and merchants through the Kingdom of Kongo and the surrounding Luanda and Mayombe. We can hypothesize that, with the assimilation of the members who migrated from the inland regions (e.g., Kasai, homeland of the Lunda and Kuba) to the culture of the coastal inhabitants, the survival of this rhythmic organization in its more fixed nature became impossible—one of the reasons why it was confined to the region from where the members were assimilated into the society.

Example 7 is the chorus of a song very popular among the Luba, to which are added various large texts according to the situation, an improvisational practice assimilated from incantation rituals and social meetings. In this version of a social meeting, the text is as follows:

Mamu yo	Mother
Mamu yo, yo...	Mother
Banu ba maluvu-a-kapia	Drinkers of rum
Kabena dikanda	Have no strength

Converted into music, the pattern clearly indicates the divisions of time that correspond to the separations marked on the transcription to facilitate reading of the score and the analysis.

Its implementation is done by beats of the hand (*bikashi*) duplicated by a basket rattle (*dikásá*) which also stresses the whole cycle without variation in the song. The beat continues in score and often is given by tamborims (*mutumbi*), sometimes doubled by the main drum (*ditumba*), before it enters the virtuosity of improvisation around the basic rhythmic cycle in discussion.

Ex. nº 8

Luba Oral Tradition

In Example 8, "Dibwe diambula kabanda," which is sung by women to accompany the bride to the home of her husband, is also an excerpt from the chorus preceded by a recitative verse. More than once, as in the first example, the subdivision metric is well emphasized by the cycle given by rattle and beat of the hand, and the beat is still marked in *mutumbi*, temporarily duplicated by the main drum.

Ex. n° 9
Dibwe diambula kabanda

In the following example, "Wa mpamba wa bitole" is a situational song sung in ceremonies of twin births or any other ceremony related with these children. During the ceremony, at the time when obscenity in public is allowed, the song is sung in responsorial style with the main singer in the middle of the circle made by dancers and singers around the musicians. While playing and singing, both the bell player and the main singer (sometimes the same person) will dance counter-clockwise in relation to the circle. Unlike the last songs, the pattern of the cycle is in its augmented form covering two time lines that corresponds to a segment of melodic line divided into "call" and "response" patterns as indicated by a solid line in the score. However, the principle of operation is the same and the instruments, to which the pattern is confined, are the same as those of all the recent examples. One small difference noted here is in doubling the basic pattern by dancers whose feet tapping follows the structure of the pattern. The common practice alongside the music and *bampamba* dance is also the same that Paulinho da Viola noted as being characteristics of rhythmic pattern in the precursor *samba* dance (see Example 9).

Example 9
"Mpamba wa Bitole"
(Transcribed by the author)

In view of the foregoing analysis, it is reasonable to suspect the Bantu rhythmic pattern could have been introduced in Brazilian musical expression by enslaved Bantu peoples, particularly those of the Kingdom of Kongo or from the Congo-Angola region. The date of their introduction in Brazil cannot be determined, but we must take into account the appearance of a manuscript with some forms of composed music—*lundu* and *modinha*—to which the pattern could belong, or even well before, kept in forms of folkloric musical expression before being popularized by Domingo Caldas Barbosa, both in Brazil and later in Portugal.

The diffusion of the *samba*'s rhythmic cycle was observed by musicologist Gerhard Kubik in the 1970s. His study highlighted the existence of the time division in musical cultures of the above-mentioned geographical zones of cultural interaction, i.e., the area mainly along the migratory route of the Lunda, the Kasai region to Luanda, and the homeland of the Lunda and Chokwe on both sides of the Congo-Angola border. Specifically, Kubik talks about the rhythmic pattern commonly used in Angola among the Luvales musicians, near Kazombo; among the Luchazi musicians in the district of Kabompo, Zambia, which refer to the pattern as *kachacha*; and in the southern Congo. As observed, this diffusion does not rely so much on their bipartite structure, which is composed of two unequal motifs consisting of nine quavers (2 +2 +2 +1 +2) and seven quavers (2 +2 +1 +2), as does the number sixteen on its basic constituent pulsations.

In comparison, the pattern observed by Kubik has the following structure, considering the placement of accents and proposing the division of the bipartite pattern which groups the pulsations is in an order opposite from *samba*:

kachacha:

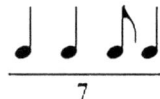

samba:

Notably, as revealed by our fieldwork in Congo, two versions of this division of time into sixteen pulses can be found in the Kasai region, mainly among the Luluwa and the Chokwe. They use the rhythmic repertoire panel of funeral songs, as illustrated in the transcription of Example 10, while among Luluwa it is the division of time for the majority of vocal and instrumental parts without any confinement to particular category. Among Luluwa, we can detect the use of both patterns. This is similar to the *samba* and another totally different structural organization of its motifs, despite the global subdivision of pulses (7 + 9). This, too, was used as a precursor of the modern music of Congo.[117]

Samba:

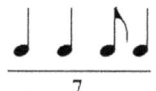

Variant Luluwa:

Tshibola

Example 10
"Tshibola Mulumbayi"
(Transcribed by the author)

In the majority of musical cultures along the West African coast, another bipartite time division pattern with twelve pulses (and its variants) was observed among the Yorùbá of Nigeria, the Akan of Ghana, and the Fon in Togo. In each of these musical cultures, variants can be grouped into three types based mainly on the organization of its structural rhythmic motifs:

1. 5 + 7:

2. 7 + 5:

3. 7 + 5:

Yet another time division pattern of twelve pulses is mentioned by Jones as being common in Central Africa and he suggests its additive aspect as follows: "We've noticed that it means a sentence of twelve quavers length, subdivided into 2 + 2 + 3: 2 + 3 or 2 + 3: 2 + 2 + 3."[118] This subdivision presents yet another structural variant, "7 + 5":

As can be observed in the above description, the patterns of division of time pulses (twelve or sixteen pulses) represent a group of possible arrangements for its component units. In other words, we have concrete examples of what we previously established on the diffusion of cultural elements and the subsequent emergence of a new stylistic trait as a result of local-regional impact on the originally adapted element. Without assigning the division of time of sixteen pulses to any specific society, we must be allowed to think that: (1) It originated from the Bantu area in general and the area of cultural interaction in particular; and (2)

although the structure of *samba* cannot be exactly allocated to a given society, or even to the place where it is practiced in Congo, we reveal here sufficient evidence from the Kasai region suggest that structure reached the west central African coast and the Americas with the forced migration of the Lunda and the Chokwe.

As far as the instrumental resources are concerned, a large number of musical instruments constitute elements of cultural unification among the societies that occupy different geographic spaces due their wide distribution across black Africa. This set of geographical spaces is what Nketia considered zones of cultural interaction. He concluded that the distribution of instrument types and musical traces across more extensive areas suggests that the musical cultures of African societies were not isolated but juxtaposed and influenced each other.[119] According to Nketia, among other instruments, there are xylophones whose use extends across the continent from east to west through the Niger–Congo linguistic area and its borders.[120]

Another idiophone instrument, which can safely be included in the category of unifying elements, is found in the *mbira*, whose use extends predominantly in mining areas in Zimbabwe, Shaba, Tanzania, and South Africa. As to its origin, G. Kubik writes, "A comparison of oral tradition of different societies, for different indigenous designations of lamelofone, based on the ethnographic literature and the typical regions of expansion, shows that the *likembe* type of lamelofone was invented some 100 or 250 years before in Katanga (Shaba–Congo) or in the north of Zambia. Thereafter, the instrument gradually spread in all directions. The *likembe* type appeared some sixty years ago in East Africa. In regions of southwestern Central African Republic, it might have been introduced between 1920 and 1930. In the region of Longa–Kwito–Kwanavale it appeared, according to the indigenous people, only some ten years ago, while the other types of lamelofone are known there for centuries. The *likembe* is still in the process of expansion in Angola, where many regions have not yet adopted this musical instrument."[121]

Categorizing the xylophone types played in African societies according to their organological traits, Nketia describes the xylophone which is made of keys mounted on a wooden frame, beneath which are suspended several gourd resonators graduated in size relative to tones of wooden blades.[122] He classifies it as the third type, which corresponds to that found on the northern coast of São Paulo, both in the neighborhood of São Francisco and in Guaratinguetá. Although this instrument is not commonly used by the Bakongo, their presence in the culturally united area is ensured by Chokwe of Angola and by the Bende, among whom a specimen of seventeen keys of the third type is found. If we have to rely on observations of number of keys, then the *marimba* specimen of ten keys found in São Francisco would have its equivalent among the Chopi of Mozambique, who also belong to the Bantu linguistic family.

The common and tuned idiophone, the *mbira*, also features a group of varieties within the same region; these varieties can be categorized based on organological representation, tuning system, or technique of touch and orchestration. In the Bakongo society, the instrument must have been introduced by the Yaka who assimilated during seventeenth century or by internal explorers. Much later, foreign acoustic practice was found embedded in sets along with a variety of percussion instruments. In Kasai, on the contrary, *mbira* of various sizes are associated with the *mákásá* (woven basket rattles), a set known as *bisanji*, such as Kadima Nseji or Kabala. In those sets, it is worth noting the role of a percussion instrument such as the main drum (a large drum of low tone), which is played by a large *mbira*, often played on a clay bowl placed in the opposite side, or else a half gourd to amplify the sound.

If we define the area of cultural interaction based on the distribution of a given musical instrument, the area covered by beaten and shaken idiophones, such as the metal bells, probably extend beyond the area covered by tuned idiophones. Note that the double bell without a clapper, known by different names in different places, has a wide distribution both among the Bantu and among the Sudanese. Note also that their size varies from one region to another. Nketia mentions that in Ghana, among the Asante, three of the larger sizes are used for some ritual music. In this, the set consists of a pair of big drums known by the name *frontonfron*.[123] Francis Bebey, on the other hand, emphasizes the use of four pairs of similarly sized bells by Bumun of Cameroon, together with a drum.[124]

At the end of the last century, the frequent use of a metal instrument known as *rubembe* was observed by Major Dias de Carvalho among the Chokwe and the Lunda, in addition to the region of Kasai. The specimens observed by the author during that period had the following dimensions: "The branches of horseshoe are two long and narrow vessels tapering towards the bow, which has a diameter of 0.010 m to 0.016 m; the opening at the ends have an oval shape, with the major axis of 0.04 m to 0.05 m and the height of vessels of 0.25 m to 0.30 m. The vessel walls are slightly thickened and strengthened by a few rims in same plane inside and outside, who meet the bow of the horseshoe."[125] Within the state of Muatiânvua, however, Carvalho observed yet another larger *rubembe* that occupies a special place in meetings.

In Congo, the same metal idiophone is also found in different sizes and is known by various names. In Kasai, it is called *nkobu* and commonly used during ceremonies for twins, the invocation of ancestors, and the expulsion of evil spirits by a traditional healer. Sometimes another bell with clapper is used in the same circumstances. Among the Bakongo, this bell is called *ngongi*, and its function extends both to the meeting and the social rituals, providing basic rhythmic patterns and contributing a harmonic rhythm, due to the sequential pattern of its low and high tones.

The instruments discussed above, therefore, do not represent a Bantu domain exclusively, but some main instrumental resources that belong or define areas of cultural interaction in Africa. It is logical to think that even if the idiophone was not introduced directly to Brazil by the enslaved Congo peoples, its presence in the Congo-Angola region greatly contributed to its survival in the Americas by helping to place these instruments among the common cultural denominators. Thus, we can include such instruments in our list of Bantu contributions. In the Americas, those who could not find the same kind of extra-musical activities put them aside over the course of time. This is the case of *sanza*, which was used in the initial years of transatlantic slaving and gradually disappeared with the advent of intensive agriculture and especially with the rise of mining in Brazil. Still others such as the *marimba* hardly survived and were confined to a specific practice, while others such as the *agogô* continued to play their roles, becoming commonplace both in musical and popular rituals.

While the above instruments have a wide distribution and virtually serve the same function among most African societies, those of the Congo Basin, which we will discuss below, define narrower areas of cultural interaction. In spite of their scattered appearances in various musical cultures, they are more concentrated in certain regions where they have acquired a particular ethical value, and are associated with ceremonies that mark the rhythm of life in society, or invoke the society's protector spirits.

One of these instruments is the woven basket rattle, classified among the varieties of container rattles, and known in Brazil by name of *caxixi*. This rattle has the form of an inverted local basket (with a narrower base than the upper part) made of reed, which is known in the Kasai region as *tshisaka* and is indispensable for carrying agricultural products. It has a handle on the top and in some local-regional variants the basket's base is reinforced with a piece of tin that contributes to acoustic amplification.

The distribution of the woven basket rattle—*díkásá*, pl. *mákásá*—is very rare in African societies, and in Congo it is mainly concentrated in the region of Kasai, which it could have only reached the coastal area through the Congo-Angola and neighboring regions. Among the Luba, it was initially associated with ceremonies for twins, but with time, began to assume the role of the gourd rattle in several other circumstances such as *bipwidi*, *madimba*, and *bisanji*, belonging to the social group in consideration. An instrument of similar material, but smaller in size, is also known among some societies in Benin, where it is called *asan*. Among the Kuba, the same instrument is used in initiation ceremonies for boys and girls, along with the friction drum (to be discussed below). In these ceremonies, all the instruments involved are covered with raffia as a way to incorporate an essential spiritual significance. The photo below shows the *díkásá* before and after preparation for the initiation ceremony among the Kuba in Lubumbashi.

On the other hand, among the Bakongo, the *díkásá* was replaced by a rattle can (locally made can containing dried seeds), which even took the traditional name of the basket rattle known in this society as *nsaka*, having the same meaning as that in the Kasai region. In lower Congo, as in most of the coastal areas where the Portuguese influence was much greater, this instrument infiltrated practically all imaginable cultural ceremonies. Its diffusion is notable among the Bakongo which, according to Balandier, is a linguistically complex society situated on the two banks of the river Congo, extending to the Batéké Plateau and the northern regions of Angola. The same Portuguese influence is also observable in Gabon and in Congo-Brazzaville, not only in their rattles but also in domestic utensils such as the oil lamp, whose use has persisted through time and space.

The use of musical bow in Africa seems to be mainly associated with the societies or groups belonging to the hunter-gatherer cultures widespread in Central Africa around the rainforest and savannah, mainly occupied by dispersed Bantu and Batwa peoples. The diffusion of this instrument among societies with other types of activities occurred later, due to multiple contacts between them. However, the wide distribution has generated a large variation in the instrument; it differs both in size and shape, contains or lacks the resonance box (that is either fixed or mobile), or is executed in a group or by an individual.[126]

It is very difficult to indicate the origin of the *berimbau* among the Bantu. However, examining the musical cultures of the coastal regions, there is a large number of musical bows whose description may well suggest the original form from which the Brazilian model could have been derived. The use of the musical bow among the Bantu in Angola was observed by Kubik, who studied its influence on its neighbors, the Kung. He notes, "*Kambulumbumba* is a Bantu word. In one or another variant, it is scattered in many cultural Bantu of Angola. The root, *mbulumbumba*, common to the names of various forms of musical bow, has existed for centuries in Angola."[127] The presence of the instrument in other societies or similar neighboring regions would be considered an adaptation by their members. Among the Mbwela, Ganguela, and the Luchazi, the division of rhythmic time in twelve pulses exists, and also in the southwest among the Kung in Kwando Kubango and the Humbi and Handa, where the term *embulumbumba* is used to denote the gourd bow. Geographically, the area of its predominance is slightly out of the zone of cultural unity, but its influence can be observed in the Luvale area and even among the Chokwe, who could have adopted it later.

Regardless of the instrument's regional variation, there is a similarity in implementation techniques that can be attributed to the size of the instrument, which requires one end to be secured on the ground. Kubik describes the instrument of individual performance, where the player often uses the mouth as resonator, as follows: "The player takes a hunting bow string and divides the rope in two unequal parts by means of a loop. This embraces the support and the rope.... For tuning, the loop is placed in such a way that the two parts of the rope produce sounds separated by the second, third or lower third largest interval....During the execution, the left hand grabs the support while the lower end of the bow supports on the floor, the top is placed in the mouth and pressed against the inside of the right side".[128]

As far as the oral bow is concerned, which uses the fixed gourd, it is secured diagonally with the end on the floor or resting on the knee of the player. During the execution, the musician continuously balances the gourd; sometimes bringing to within a few millimeters of the skin of the breast, and then moving it away. By means of this technique the vibratory resonator is altered, becoming the source of a little audible harmonic melody.[129] In the implementation of the bow as part of a group, the string holder joins a clay bowl upside-down on the floor, or to one-half of a large gourd. One end of the bow is secured below with the left foot by one of the performers. The arc is placed so that the rope is high, while the support rests partly on the sandy floor while it is pressed against the resonator.[130]

Out of these three types that are used within the same society and their neighbors, the instrument with the resonator seems to have a more earlier form than the modified version, that exists in Brazil. First, the size of the bow does not allow the instrument to be secured in a vertical position; second, this trait has been reduced. The bow is used without the metal ring or *caxixi*, and in Brazil, these elements characterize the local-regional versions. Some noteworthy similarities can be found in the technical use of the resonator and particularly in musical material. In a private conversation with Kubik, he played some recordings of a musical bow recorded in Angola, where we could observe similarities with the patterns used in Bahia by *capoeira* players.

It should not be stressed that the *berimbau*, as it is known today in Brazil, did not come from Africa, but drew its model from several popular music bows in the Bantu area where transatlantic slaving was practiced. What is more interesting is the survival of musical material that has been adapted for a different function. The diffusion of this instrument in the Americas can certainly be attributed to transatlantic slaving, through which the same instrument arrived in Cuba and kept its name, as recorded by Ortiz. In Brazil, the name, which does not seem to be an African one, could also be some type of modification of the original name *mbulumbumba*.[131]

The origin of the *cuíca* and the center of its diffusion in the world have been the object of controversy since the work of Curt Sachs. The instrument is included in the last stratum corresponding to specific areas around the world. According to Sachs, the *cuíca* must have been derived from the Javanese zither monotone. He wrote, "A vibrant rope or rod, attached to the center of a membrane that covers a hole on the ground which transmits the vibrations, is one of the characteristics of flat sitar and may have been inspired by it."[132] The universality of this instrument seems to be confirmed by Oliveira; although the name of the instrument found in Brazil is of Congo-Angola origin, the instrument itself could have a simultaneous origin in other parts of the world. But suggesting a more limited area, Cascudo locates the origin of the *cuíca* among the Arabs, who might have been responsible for its spread throughout the world, including African societies.

Oliveira takes a different view, arguing, "they originated from Africa certainly because they are very common in this continent, and went to Portugal and Spain with the first wave of black Kongos in the fifteenth century when they began to import slaves in the peninsula, from Congo via Lisbon."[133] Sharing the same view, Ortiz says that the instrument could have been brought to Portugal and Spain by Africans in in fifteenth and sixteenth century Congo, and reached the rest of Europe and the Americas, directly or indirectly through the enslaved. Oliveira distinguishes two broad categories of the *cuíca*, using the the rod position as a criterion: it is either internal or external to the instrument's body. In Europe and particularly in Portugal, France, and Belgium, the characteristic trait is the external position of the rod and the techniques of playing. The instrument is secured by the arm, while the other hand manipulates the rod.

The African models, in general, are characterized by the internal position of the connecting rod as well as by the position of touch. Oliveira describes it thus: "The instrument rests on the floor with it skin facing the dance: the 'operator' also sits down on the floor with the mouth of the instrument between the legs; alternate hands, wet with water, tighten the cane from the skin to the mouth".[134]

On the African continent, the concentration of the *cuíca* and particularly internal rods seem to be limited to Bantu societies, although some exceptions of the *cuíca* with external rods were observed among the Baila of South Africa. On the other hand, among the Sudanese, the most common friction drum does not have any rod, but belongs to what Oliveira classified as direct friction, since the friction is made directly on the head of the drum. Some rare cases of *cuíca* with external rods, however, are recorded among the Bekom of northwest Cameroon.[135]

In African societies where it is used, the instrument seems to play a similar role: to symbolize the voices and value of the leopard, lion, bird, etc., according to the totemic animal of the society. Among the Kuba, for example, or among the Bakongo, the *cuíca* symbolizes the lion in the initiation camp of boys. Oliveira writes, "As a general rule, they are sacred instruments that appear in ceremonies of the catechumen's revelation of true nature of the mysterious voice that is heard during the ceremonies. They can be used during funeral rites, death of members and even during sacrifices. They are played only, by and for, the initiated, and in some cases when they are heard, the women must hide."[136] The latter situation is similarly found among the Bakuba or the Luba-Shankadi, where the drum or its substitute ("bull-roarer," a flat piece of wood on the end of a rope, which makes a resounding noise when whirled) is played to announce the return of the newly initiated to the village. On that occasion, the women have to hide.

In Congo, the instrument seems to have been first known in the Kingdom of Kongo, where it must have reached some of the interior societies, especially the Kuba, with whom it came into contact. Its limited regional use can be traced back to the migratory route of the Kuba—from the Kingdom of Kongo to the current land of the Kuba—that includes all the regions of Kuango-Kuilu and a part of the Kasai region. This is confirmed through the use of the "bull-roarer" by some societies in Kasai for the same functions that are performed by the *cuíca*, among the Kuba and the Bakongo.

Limiting the issue to the Congo-Angola area, it is clear that the instrument has been known for centuries among its cultural groups. Its diffusion to the Iberian Peninsula must be attributed, in part, to the presence of so many members of the Congolese court who spent some time studying in Portugal since the latter half of the fifteenth century. At the beginning of the sixteenth century, the enslaved peoples from the Kongo served in Portugal for a considerable period before arriving in Brazil and other parts of the Americas. The Portuguese soldiers, merchants and farmers could also very well have transplanted the general idea of the instrument into their local European countries where it is known under local-regional names, such as *sarroncas, zambomba, adufe*, etc.[137]

In conclusion, on the origin of the principle of the *cuíca* and its possible global channels of diffusion, Oliveira seems to share our conviction when he writes, "The fact that it [the friction drum] has been widely used in Spain by the Moors does not contradict this thesis because the Moors could have received it from blacks. On the other hand, the assertion of Aranzandi that a zambomba in Spain is a popular urban tool and not for peasants, is not contradicted by the 'populace of Madrid,' because there were many black slaves who had urban jobs and they would use the zambombas in the Christmas festivities."[138] But Oliveira goes on further to say, "Ortiz and these authors apparently are unaware of gothic sarronca figuration of fifteenth century Spain, sculpted in the steps of the choir of Santa Maria de Morella in València. There, one sees a shepherd playing the instrument together with a 'naciemento,' which certifies its existence in Spain prior to the immigration of black people from Kongo, on the basis of the findings."

Although we have not personally examined the aforementioned evidence in order to take a position on the matter, an easy adaptation or assimilation of the instrument before new forms were allowed to emerge and which were organologically different from their original is also quite possible. The time period under discussion includes the arrival of members of the Kongo court or enslaved Bakongo individuals and when the sculpture of the "sarronca" could have been made in the same century. Therefore, as Oliveira indicates, the Bakongo *kinfwiti* (which became the Brazilian friction drum, the *cuíca*) and the European sarronca" could not have shared the same place of origin.[139] In short, and in spite of its use by the eastern and western Bantu, it is probable the model of the Brazilian friction drum—the *cuíca*—could have been introduced to Brazil by enslaved Africans of the Congo-Angola region. It is also possible the Portuguese or Spaniards strengthened the principle of the instrument to ensure its survival through the ruling class of the new society, although the organological structure remained from its originating societies but whose members were the new lower class.

PART III
MUTATION, PERSISTENCE, AND CONTINUITY

CHAPTER 4

CONCEPTUAL MUTATION AND
BANTU MUSICAL ELEMENTS IN THE
POPULAR TRADITIONS OF BRAZIL

The trend of examining "mutation," as a state of transformation or passage in the field of sociological research, began to crystallize since the second half of the 1960s by members of the Association Internationale des Sociologues de Langue Française (AISLF). The term was already common, however, in the twelfth century among jurists to qualify a certain order of change. For French philosopher Auguste Comte, the same term began to gain new emphases of "change" and "resistance," as continuities of social structures or cultural elements. According to Karl Marx, studies of society formed the basis for the "transformation" of a society, but when limited writings from members of the AISLF were observed, it became apparent that the aspect of "mutation" emphasized by French language sociologists was on drastic changes arising out of a "revolutionary" action. Edgar Morin noted, at a colloquium on "mutation," that "it is the aspect of the revolution that dominates this colloquium on mutation, and even the concept of mutation."[140] For Georges Balandier, "The term mutation [in the sociological sense] falls into a broad semantic field where the terms are in some way similar: change, evolution, revolution, development, modernization, etc.," all loaded with ambiguity. All these forms serve to express the differences that appear with respect to strict repetition (or reproduction) of social forms, while some emphasize the persistence of a fundamental identity despite the apparent amendments and *rupture*.[141]

According to Roger Bastide, "mutation" came to designate the principle of severance in the social sciences.[142] But Bastide qualifies this statement: "We won't talk of mutation while being in the same structure; we will reserve this term for any change which is defined as the passage of a structure to another, such as revolution of 'systems.'"[143] In other words, as Balandier describes it, mutation is composed of "the changes that ensure the *passage* of a social structure to another, of a system of structures to another."[144]

Unlike these authors, with whom we partially share the mutation concept, the changes in social structure for us occur after a conditioning of the nucleus in which they are designed prior to their realization. This conditioning is established on the principle of *rupture,* which, in turn, is generated in the principle of severance. The concept of rupture does not mean an action or an event (revolution, war, slavery, etc.), but a phenomenon resulting from an action, in this case one that separates an ideology of ethical values (i.e., cultural identity) from which it draws its life and meaning. This disturbance of traditional order in the core of culture by severance is the one to which Bastide referred in his statement as a disorder and which Edgar Morin called a "crisis," in that "the crisis can cause a mutation and the mutation is often linked to a crisis."[145] For Morin, "What draws the attention in crisis—a phenomenon of rupture—is something that springs from it," and that something is "mutation."[146]

Viewed from the above perspective, a new aspect of mutation, in addition to those proposed by Morin, can be formulated.[147] It lies mainly at the level of conceptualization, i.e. where the conceived element or cultural practice is assigned the symbolic value of a cultural trait in their designers' society. At this level of consideration, the mutation does not necessarily cause change in the direct structure as applied to the study of social change, but mainly affects the level of design and structure while leaving it intact. A similar consideration is also found in Levi-Strauss's theory in the analysis of social structure by Radcliffe-Brown. Levi-Strauss distinguishes two different levels: the theoretical and the practical. The first reinforces our interest because it is a level of expression where the concepts are formulated in their greatest extent and away from what gives them meaning and existence.[148]

Although conditioned by imbalance resulting from rupture (e.g., crisis, revolution), the action or process of mutation is not necessarily as abrupt as the members of the AISLF desire, but gradually supplied by the necessity of survival, or better, by the principle of existence. This manifests in the persistence of cultural elements outside the traditional core as retained in the individual and collective memories of their bearers. In short, the new aspect of mutation is thus described at the formal level to the extent that it only affects the *psyche*, and indirectly the *society*. It is only in this context we can consider our concept of mutation as sharing Herskovits's principle of reinterpretation, and Bastide's notion of acculturation.

In contrast to some of the anthropological theories aimed at studying reality as a *principle* or *concept* and not as a *system*, structuralism and functionalism are most helpful in defining the relationship of cultural and musical elements studied as entities within their functional societies (e.g., secret societies, families, ceremonial repertoires, etc.). In a complementary way, the methodology of mutation stresses the *passage* not as an evolution or continuity, but as a shift of conceptual levels, making the same idea and structures (e.g., musical rudiments) shift from "traditional" to "popular." In this line of thought, it is assumed that the mutation (applied here as the changing levels of conception) of a product of human behavior is strongly influenced by phenomena of life that affect not only the produced behavior (thus determining its tendency to develop) as demonstrated by humans, but also begins its action on the psychic core, where the behavior is designed. Thus, the main methodological concern should be directed not at the musical material itself, but at revealing the nature of the determinants and analyzing the action of the latter in the core of the human psyche.

Using Bastide terms, the determinants are divisible into two main categories: "external causality," the action exerted by social means, and "internal causality," the transforming action associated with the individual psyche.[149] For his part, Balandier summarizes the same determinants in as "internal dynamic" and "external dynamic," which Mantle Hood calls "manufacturers of musical consensus"—three sets of rules that govern our present interest, the psychic core from which human behavior is conceived.[150] Thus, in the words of A. Merriam, "The music is a product of man and has structure, but its structure can't have an existence independent from the behavior that the produces it. In order to understand why a musical structure exists in a certain way, we must also understand how and why the concepts that form the basis of this behavior are ordered in such a way as to produce a desired particular form of organized sound."[151]

Our notion of conceptual mutation share concerns that students of social mutation have, as well as that expressed by Balandier: "In order to arrive at this last point (explanation of the phenomena of social change), there is still the longest part of the journey: the demand of the determinants of the mutation, assuming in beginning that they may join different formulas... from which the mutation drags the [entire] society with its movement..."[152] These "different formulas" can certainly be interpreted as cultures and traditions, which are the primary determinants of the behavior of the individual, as well as the concept that the individual has of him or herself.[153] They are probably the basis of the "cultural psychology" that Bastide mentions but avoids discussing in his essay on formal acculturation. Bastide wrote, "But we can't generalize from the case of the child where there is development, maturation, brief progress, even acculturation; each culture has its value, all placed consequently in the same levels, none constituting a step in some progress. It is the cultural psychology that we should ask for information about the question."[154]

It is important to define the semantic limits of terms such as "traditional" and "popular" for the purposes of this chapter. By "traditional," we mean to a well-established continuity, whose mere existence is vitalized by ideological concepts governed by standards and values. What is traditional belongs to a fixed group—a family, a society, a cultural group, etc. On the definition of tradition, Balandier argued, "The notion of tradition has a broad sense and its acceptance is, often, vague. In its most common definition, in conformity with the socially prescribed rules of conduct, in adherence to the specific order of society and culture in question, and in the refusal or inability to conceive an alternative, it implies to do away with the 'commandments' which were valid for the past."[155] But tradition sometimes operates within the collective and individual consciousness, and within the constitutive relations of social life.

On the other hand, "popular" refers to the new state of a tradition taken out of vital context, thus losing what was identifiable to a specific cultural group. In other words, what is popular would be traditional, except for the absence of what gives them particular a meaning and existence. Balandier says that this is in conformity with the rules of conduct laid down by the society and breaks the "commandments" which were valid for the past. Likewise, "popular" here refers to a traditional concept that has become commonplace among societies or even nations.

The organization of cultural communities among the Bantu in the Congo Basin, as found in the majority of African societies, are based on the interaction of social and ritual groups such as secret societies and societies of puberty rites. Each one of these societies have particular rules and practices extracted from common area of resources—cultural traditions—which is involved in its preservation. On these terms, we must treat these societies as functional within the context of culture.

In music, diversities and similarities are revealed in the use of musical instruments and in the organization of the raw material (e.g., musical melody contour, harmonic implication, rhythmic interpolation, even the hierarchy of the catalog of notes). On one hand, in a cultural community, one can speak of a musical instrument or material belonging to a given functional society or to a ceremony with which it is associated. On the other hand, the similarities of the same elements among societies or functional ceremonies act as links that strengthen the interaction among the constituent segments of the cultural community organization. But examining only the divergence of musical traces, each repertoire, set, or composition can be used to identify their respective society or ceremony function, reflecting its stylistic musical models.[156] These models together, married with the existing similarities, define the characteristic criteria of "ethnic" musical culture.

This is the case with the set of Bantu musical traces detected between rhythmic patterns and musical instruments and, in general, defines the musical traits of Luba society, and is specifically identifiable with functional societies within the larger society. On one hand, there is the following example, which is the basis of the majority of the *bampamba* songs and is rarely adapted to the accompaniment of songs from the repertoire and other categories:

The function of the time division in *bampamba* could only be defined by informants as determining the *díkàsà dià májá* (the dance step). But we should deepen our observation by verifying the relationship of *díkàsà dià májá* with the position it occupies within the ceremony. The *bampamba* ceremony, the initial part is made inside the house involving only the interested parties and concludes the ceremony with the participation of the public. The invocation is commonly performed with the dance (*díkàsà dià májá*) even if it is made with a mere accompaniment of a simple iron bell with a clapper, known among the Luba as *nkobu*, performed by the celebrant. In other ceremonies, in addition to the *bampamba* among the Luba, a similar function of invocation is not attributed to the simple constituent unit of musical expression that generates the set of words, the rhythmic patterns, the instrumentation, and the dance steps. In other words, an invocation of spirits or the expulsion of evil in the *bampamba* ceremony involves the total expression as detailed above, including the correct props and the traditionally known celebrant. Therefore, when an informant emphasizes the fact that this rhythmic pattern determines only the dance step, he or she means that the pattern itself is not functional.

In this context, the rhythmic pattern in consideration receives its meaning when incorporated into the total expression. In addition to its purely musical function to determine the length of the melodic contour and the length of the constituent part of the song, this invocational rhythmic pattern has a role to fulfill.

A similar story is seen with the *díkàsà* (basket rattle), which is also identified with the *bampamba* ceremony among the Luba, and slightly modified among the Kuba to become one of the special features of the puberty rites for boys. In both cases, the role of the *díkàsà* is twofold. On one hand, it provides the basic rhythmic pattern, while on other hand its extra-musical function—as a part of the ceremonial headdresses—must not be discounted.

Before being incorporated into the *bampamba* ceremony for the first time, there is a blessing of the *díkàsà*, during which a small libation or *diedi dia lupemba* is made at the bottom of the instrument as a symbol of its sacred function. Unlike the Luba, in the puberty rite of Kuba boys, the *díkàsà* has a mythical significance assigned to it by traditional practice. At this occasion, probably the only time when it is used among the Kuba, the instrument is covered with raffia to prevent the uninitiated from seeing it. Thus, whatever role the instrument represented within this society, its symbolic value assumes significance when found within the totality of the expression regulated by ritualistic patterns. In other words, outside of the whole situation in which the instrument is an integral part, or in terms of Brandel, a tool, it loses the value assigned to it by tradition for a given ceremony and assumes a modified meaning or a completely new use.[157]

In the context of Luba tradition, the concept of assigned value seems to be determined and protected by at least two standards of traditional culture derived from cultural practices. The first of them—the sense of belonging—is derived from the essence of the identity that is based on the philosophy of Bantu identification.[158] It is the state of being an integral part of the total invocation, which generates other phenomena—such as the site of their related traits (e.g., trees, rivers), props, music and others—within which any of the constituents derive their value and ethical meaning. Without these or with its modification, the invocation may lose their effectiveness, regardless of its nature. Bastide underscores a similar idea in his essay on why the Bantu religion based on ancestors did not survive in the Americas, as in the case of its Sudanese counterpart. Bastide writes, "The basis was their veneration of ancestors;…slavery broke the lineages and they dispersed, making it impossible for the veneration of lineage. Still it is necessary to add that along with the spirits of certain rivers, forests and mountains of Africa, they were located in a well-defined fragment of land and were impossible to be driven into exile. Here we have reasons that weigh heavily against the perpetuation of Bantu regilion in [the] America[s]."[159]

In music, Brandel puts it this way, "The psychological etiology here is the power and efficiency. The instruments—an integral part of magic and religion and music is such instrument—need to have some permanent sacred way to play their roles with the greatest efficiency."[160] Valuable example, found within the repertoire of songs sung by Luba-Shankadi girls during the *butanda* (a period of female initiation), reflect the Bantu concept of dual identity, marked by the rite which symbolizes the death of the child and the birth of the adult.

In these songs (see Examples 11, 12 and 13), there are two singers in terms of structure.[161] But, as you can see, the role of the second singer is not essential in musical terms because he or she repeats exactly the first half of the song sung by the first singer. When the chorus enters with the melodic sequence of the second half of the first singer's material, in the majority of the repertoire's songs, the sequence starts at the interval of third major above the original note. At the end of each sequence, there is an elaboration of the second original motif. As interpreted among the Luba, the reflected dual identities are of a "child" in the second singer and an "adult" in the choir. Both are represented in a single person who is the first singer. This double description of child and adult along with the notions of death and birth are the philosophy reflected in the cultural musical structure of songs sung during the period of initiation referred to above. In other words, this musical structure has meaning only when examined in the light of its entire extra-musical sphere, for which or in which it is conceived. In this way, we must treat this structure as belonging only to ceremonial rites, as conceived by the Luba-Shankadi.

CHAPTER 4

Naya twa Mboko
Ex. nº 12

Song taken from Kazadi, P.C. *The characteristic criteria in the vocal music of the Luba-Shankadi children*

Munuma ne Mukaji
Ex. nº 13

Kiluwe kya Mulongo Malato
Ex. nº 14

Here, we provide another example to demonstrate the importance of ownership as the supreme determinant and protective value to which musical rudiments are traditionally assigned. It is found in *nyimbu ya kusansula* and other kinds of orature (e.g., poetry, elegy). Its structural patterns are determined by cultural consideration such as the philosophy of life after death (which is manifested in the name of children), while revealing another aspect of the dual identity of the Bantu. The first, which we prefer to call a spiritual identity or representative, depends on the ancestor's name, its emphasis on the family lineage, and the merits of the deceased. The other, that which we call physical identity, determines concrete phenomena such as the land, mountains, rivers, physical appearance, and in this way constituting the primary entity of the *muntu* (the whole living being). These are the same identities that Bastide expressed respectively as "temporal continuity" (ancestral presentation) and "spatial diversity" (e.g., location of souls, privileged relations with certain places, objects, geniuses, etc.).[162]

In the first identity, there is a culturally defined division of labor such as hereditary function, that is, those functions inherited by a person from the ancestor of the family whose name he or she preserves; and hierarchical function, those functions performed by an individual due to the position he or she occupies within a family. The last function is determined mainly by age, sex, and kinship. In the last identity, *muntu* gives a symbolic value to all the phenomena of his or her biotope (in which he or she lives). For example, *kabundi* (the family antelope) is found in majority of the tales of the Luba as a symbol of intelligence; likewise, the lion's share symbolizes wisdom, and the leopard symbolizes good luck. The mountains, anthills, rivers, and forests are regarded as the villa of protective spirits of the society. Not only do they admire other animals for their ferocity and strength, but also symbolically compete with them for magically desirable traits.[163]

The repertoire of Luba-Shankadi children is a valuable source of songs that illustrate the subject matter discussed above.[164] One song from that repertoire, *Tata Mwalaba*, reads:

> *Tata mwalaba*
>
> Father who lives in the other banks of the Lualaba river
>
> *Mpeko bwato nkalonde nyama*
>
> Give me a canoe to fish
>
> *Wa kobeya*
>
> You, in whose house fish swim
>
> *Matenta a nkanga*
>
> You, the head of a big family
>
> *Tata wadi wa Bantu*
>
> Father who is surrounded by many people.

Here we are not talking anything about the physical appearance of the father. All praise is for the things with which the father is identified, i.e. things that belong to him or to which he belongs, which in this case are the land and the family, illustrating spatial diversity.

Although a married woman goes to the village of her husband after the marriage, in cultural functions, such as in ceremonies invoking ancestors of the family, she is considered a foreign element, both in the family of her husband and the new family unit formed by her husband and herself. In the patrilineal system of Luba society, where children follow the male's (father's) line of descent and regardless of the length of marriage, she will continue to be the daughter of her family of origin where she has the right to participate in all rites of the family. To the family of her husband, she is the "daughter of others." Thus, the quality of a family member for the Bantu is an important aspect of identification on a spiritual level. In the following example taken from the repertoire of Luba infants, we will notice the wording of the identity of this "daughter of others":

Mwana bene

Daughter of others (other people's daughter)

Wa kabaya ka mutoma Nkongolo

She wants to hold the bowl of water
reserved only for Nkongolo's family

Kimanyi Kyo kyavwele

She is dressed in precious clothes

Kyangala kya kashi bulembu

The appearance of it evokes the inner sweetness

Mwana bene

Daughter of others (other people's daughter)

Au wenda washiye ntanda

Then she goes leaving terrestrial life.

Her name is not taken but her identity is composed primarily by the quality of her family, whether figurative or imaginary. Structurally, it is only after the first two verses speaking of her family identity that the *muntu* believes in making a physical description of the praised. In this case it is an elegy to a deceased woman.

The next song is taken from the repertoire of popular music from Congo. In this self-praise song, the composer emphasizes nothing more than the personal pride he feels as a member of the Bayeke village (see also Example 15):

Masanga

Example 15
"Masanga"
(Jean Bosco Mwenda. Transcribed by the author, 1974)

Nani namwenda njiva yetu Jadotville

Anyone traveling to Jadotville

Upitiyue njiya yetu ya Buluo

Passing by Buluo

Umwambiye Baba Bosco wa Bayeke

Speak to Baba Bosco wa Bayeke

Umwambiye ende akalale kwabo

Tell him to go sleep at home

On the other hand, it is still in urban music of Congo as *Belela authenticité na kati ya congress* ("acclaim authenticity in the congress"), composed by Lwambo "Franco" Makiadi, a verse that sums up the essence of the principle of belonging:

Soki nakeyi mboka mosusu

In a foreign country

Mopaya atuni ngai ekolo na ngai

And a stranger asks "Who am I?"

Na motindo na ngai

In my own way

Na lolendo na ngai na koyebisa ye

Proudly I will answer him

Ngai Zairois

I am Zairian

Parti na ngi M.P.R.

My political party is M.P.R.

Mokonzi na ngai Mobutu Sese Seko

My "chief" is Mobutu Sese Seko.

In this song, the proud answer to the question, "Who am I?"— in other words what is my true identity—is marked by land, family and father. These elements are represented in the song in national terms: (1) land—Zaire/Congo; (2) family—Popular Movement of the Revolution, defined by its founder president politically organized as a country; (3) father—Mobutu Sese Seko, President of the Republic. It should be noted that the individual does not mention his name but the cultural values by which he is identified. The argument around the principle of identity can also be detected in the concept of "person" among several African societies. Despite the nature of the identity, i.e. temporal continuity or spatial diversity in which the African "I" is inserted, the principle of belonging seems to be a source of vital significance. For the African, the being is conceived as a constitutive element of the cosmos created by his community, his society, his clan, his family, and the set of norms and values of these institutions. In this harmony of values within a cosmos, the constituent elements interact and complement one another. This underlines the belief that an African lives in a world in which all elements are related and integrated. Once outside the society, where the vital force is no longer assured, the being loses its identity, along with all that provided protection and gave meaning to its existence. In other words, if there is a disturbance in the psyche, this leads to the disorder, imbalance, and finally destruction of one's essence; the essence that can only be reestablished by returning to his or her cosmos.

In this world, music and dance function as media of communication and documentation, and serve as essential vessels for oral tradition. These media are contained in the Bantu philosophy of existence, its significance, and its embodiment in the expression, "I belong, therefore I am," or, as expressed in the Zulu term of *ubuntu*, based on the symbiotic relationship between all elements within the universe. This underlying conception of music and dance in Africa survived in Brazil because of the impact or influence of oral tradition on the individual's mind. On this point, Hampate Bâ wrote, "Oral tradition is the great school of life, all aspects of which are covered and affected by it. It is at once religion, knowledge, natural science, apprenticeship in a craft, history, entertainment, and recreation."[165]

Among the Wolof of Senegal, a person who has left the society is considered sick. To cure him, all the rites are conceptualized as a reincorporation into society, where he reenters in harmony with the values that define his vital person. And so Thomas and Luneau write in relation to masks used for this purpose: "This (mask) appears uniquely in the rites of passage and on the occasion of ceremonies with therapeutic purposes, where the group carries the patient [especially the possessed], packing him safely and tries to reintegrate him within the collectivity."[166] On the other hand, in his study *La Conception de la Personne dans la Penseé Traditionnelle Yorùbá*, I. P. Lalèyê, suggests the inseparability of the individual from his or her society:

> In the same way, to integrate the group, the rites of baptism begin thoroughly. It continues with the various stages of education and extends to the various tutorials in various moments of life. It remains the same when it comes to curing a sick person or to helping the souls of the dead make the journey that should lead them next to their ancestors. The society takes possession of the individual from his birth, marks him in various ways until his death. On the contrary, the health of his soul is not in any other part but in the link of this same society that ensures the funeral and the veneration that perhaps even divinize him. Everything happens as if the society would be able to suggest to each individual the laws that govern the life within the group and ensure its survival. These individuals compose the immediate or mediate death and physical or mental disease through their own fault (no more in harmony with other elements of his cosmos).[167]

Viewed this way, the African "I" exists only when it is framed by other elements that complement each other (society, myth, land, etc.); it is the *existence*, which is a set of *being* with all the immaterial elements that constitute his or her cosmos, and a set of critical values of his tradition that complement his identity.[168] These relationships lose their interactive values once placed outside its traditional framework.

What we refer to as the "sense of belonging" is the same which anthropologists refer to as "anthropocentrism," which considers the individual's reaction when found outside of his or her traditional setting. In short, it should not be underemphasized that the concept of belonging among the Bantu constitutes the essence of its philosophy of identity and personhood. It also occupies within this large and composite cultural grouping an important position among the determinants of the concept of attributive values, layered within cultural, clan, and family traditions. And this concept of belonging provides relevant clues about the nature of a musical model belonging to a given functional "society" or ceremony, and also set the criteria of a stylistic musical culture.

In the cultural norms that determine the values attributable to the constituent elements of society, it is noticeable that the second of the two traditional norms can certainly be a relevant component of the "division of labor" principle, which designates who should celebrate or officiate which ceremony. The ritual and ceremonial functions must be performed by a person ritually initiated or traditionally designated as such in order to maintain their effectiveness. Among the Luba, it is frequently observed that an older person in all rituals may replace a child who has inherited some function from an ancestral name, but whose presence is essential to maintaining the power of invocation. This is generally valid for the majority of the ritual functions or ceremonies with religious connotation and in which the effectiveness is the main object. We should emphasize the traditional meaning and importance attached to the functions which we called "hereditary function" and "hierarchical function."

When observed closely, the role assumed by ritually initiated individuals may not be included within the categories of functions mentioned above. Yet it belongs to another category, "function gained." This is because it does not belong to the tradition of the newly initiated (e.g., family, "ethnic") although it may be the beginning. In other words, the new celebrant does not possess any continuity. Many times, the functions of this category are exercised at the level of the cultural group and not in the family.

Returning to the musical traces, the same principle of belonging seems to prevail and the distinguished protective cultural norms are also applicable to its traditionally assigned value. This value, as already stressed in the rhythmic pattern of four pulses and the woven basket rattle (*díkàsà*), exists only in expressions that generate songs, dance, other musical instruments, and costumes worn by celebrants and participants, all belonging to the *bampamba* ceremony. A similar principle of belonging is also applicable to the time line pattern of sixteen pulses and its variant, which differs in the organization of its components:

Original:

♩ ♩ ♪♩
—7—

Variant:

♪♩ ♩ ♩ ♩
—9—

These are stylistic traits of musical cultures among clans that derived from the Luba (mainly the Luluwa and Bena Kanyoka) and its neighbors in the Kasai region. In the transcripts, these patterns are described with their ritual and social meaning in the region. The first pattern emphasizes a song sung in the graveyard among the Bena Kanyoka, while the variant coordinates musical parts of a social gathering song among the Luluwa. Therefore, the conclusions drawn for the *bampamba* musical elements are also valid for these patterns in their respective repertoires.

The musical instruments lend themselves to such an analysis on account of the diversity of their use in each respective group. On one hand, there is the *berimbau* for which there is no known document that discusses its involvement in a ceremony of any kind. G. Kubik, who contributed valuably to the literature on the Bantu in Angola, says that it could be the original of what is known in Brazil as the *berimbau* but hardly mentions the ritualistic meaning of the *mbulumbumba* instrument among the Angolan societies. Kubik does, however, mention the use of the instrument by children. He notes, "One day we discovered the execution bow in the nearby cultural groups of Bantu, the *mbwelas* and *ganguelas*. First we see it in [the village of] Chingangu and a few weeks later in Chissende. In Bantu, the bow group had become a rare child instrument."[169] Later in the same source, the author says that all these varieties of musical bows, found in use among the Kung and their Bantu neighbors, are a means of entertainment for children. Therefore, without drawing hasty conclusions, it would be safe to consider this instrument as being purely for social circumstances.

The double bell—the *agogô*—is even more difficult to analyze due to the vast area of cultural interaction it resides. In this area, which spreads over all of Africa, the value assigned to the instrument corresponds to the various roles that it traditionally plays among the constituent groups—functions that vary from ritual and social in nature or from magical to profane, depending on context, and even within the same community. Both adults and children use it to accompany their songs, and their use is not limited to one gender. Both in larger and smaller sets, it gives the basic rhythmic or contrapuntal patterns. In Brazil, the double bell is submitted to the same uses. The *agogô* is a relevant instrument accompanying the music of Candomblé, although in some backyards it is omitted. In the *samba* school, it is an essential tool and a great variety of *agogô* are industrially manufactured; the same instrument occupies a prominent position in popular musical ensembles (cf. Example 3). In this respect it is valid to talk about mutation, i.e., the change in the way of conceiving the instrument, assigning it other values in addition to those with whom it was identified in Africa. It can be said that, in spite of the change in society (from Africa to Brazil), the double bell has preserved its main functions such as those carried out in Africa, although not identically.

With the friction drum, the situation is completely different due to two major factors: (1) Its cultural interaction zone can be limited to a given geographical area that extends through the current lower Congo (including some societies from the west bank of the Congo River), the Kasai region (the land of the Kuba), passing through the land of the Yaka, the Lunda, and the Chokwe on both sides of the Congo-Angola border. In Angola, the same instrument with similar organological traits (e.g., inner rod, hollow tree trunk, etc.) is common among the Mbundu and must have been offered to their neighbors; and (2) in this zone, the friction drum appears to be associated mainly with ritual ceremonies, particularly those related to death, in the funeral place or during the initiation period that symbolizes death of the child and birth of the adult.

Among the Bakuba and the Bakongo, of which the first must have assimilated the instrument, the friction drum is seen in the initiation ceremonies where it symbolically represents the sound of the functional society's totem animal. Among the Kuba, it receives more mystical value since it is covered with raffia to prevent the group members from seeing it (as are other instruments in the set). For the Kuba, insiders believe that it represents the voice of the lion. At the end of the initiation period, the instrument is played in the village to summon the return of the new men.

In Bakongo society, where the instrument is also used in funeral ceremonies, similar symbolic values are observed since the sound of the instrument represents the voice of the deceased. It is worth noting that in Bakuba society, the friction drum is reserved for ritual purposes and is played only at the start of such events. This restriction is not observed by the Bakongo (including the Vili on other side of the Congo river, the Democratic Republic of Congo/Zaire), where women also use the instrument with the same morphological traits in their ceremonies.

A deeper look into the use of the instrument (with an inner rod), wherever it is found in the world, reveals the friction drum is still known by its Kikongo name of *kinfwiti*, and is also a prominent tool in invocations and part of what we have seen in relation to the presentation of the instrument itself within the context of the ceremony. The majority of the Bantu religious practices were transplanted in Cuba, and Ortiz notes, "In Cuba, the counterpart instrument, which has great importance among the Congo strata, takes the name of *kinfwiti*...It is played in the Congo *cabildos* [i.e., brotherhoods] with certain drums, uni-membranophones, and religious character, hidden out of sight of singers and dancers as with all fricatives, which are the voice of the Senhor do Grande Mistério, the leopard, the hurricane, the dead, or the God. It is mainly invoked in ceremonies depicting the dead, funerals, or necromancy."[170]

The *kinfwiti* maintained its original symbolic value in Cuba, and Ortiz further reveals some valuable information that confirms the persistence of Bantu practices and beliefs transplanted to the Americas. About those Kongo of Cuba, the author says, "The sound of fricative membranophones continues to be feared between blacks and whites, with the same funerary symbolism and trembling as that of in Africa. In various [religious practices] of African origin who continue to practice it in Cuba, one continues to hear the deep voice of the arcane, i.e., an esoteric rite whose sacred value imposes a terrible oath. For these Kongo, it still personifies the voice of the dead or the totemic leopard."[171]

For this instrument, the application of mutational analysis is central to our study for it clarifies the determinants of the mutation that occurred in the mind of their bearers from Africa to the Americas. In other words, although the friction drum, known in Brazil by its more popular name, *cuíca*, cannot be attributed to a given society in Africa as some scholars claim, we believe that, based on organological traces, the *cuíca* could only have been modeled according to the Bantu specimen common among the occupants of the Congo-Angola area. Although in Brazil the instrument has lost some of its main traditional tasks, it has become commonplace, though deprived of its former cultural values. How this happened will be the subject of the next chapter. We will delve into the nature of the persistence of transplanted Bantu cultural elements, already observable in Brazilian popular musical expression, especially in terms of rhythmic patterns and musical instruments.

Theorizing about the matter in comparative perspective, Ortiz gives due respect to the *kinfwiti* in Cuba and its practices in constrast to the Brazilian *cuíca*. Ortiz wrote, "The Cuban *kinfwiti* does not have the popularity of the Brazilian *puita* [*cuíca*]" because "the sound impression communicated with 'another world.' As the language of Supreme Mystery, it is something so sacred that the black Africans, their descendants, and whites, who trans-cultured their [beliefs] with the metaphysical, prevented the African instruments from criticism and apparitions in public vulgarity, trivial and profane."[172] Against this observation, one can see how beliefs, cultural values, and music were adapted by its practitioners in a particular tradition.

One can submit several relevant phenomena, such as determinants of formal mutation experience by carriers of the musical elements, for consideration. Among others, scholars who study transatlantic slaving have emphasized different facets of the diffusion and traces of African culture in the rest of the world. Some scholars have progressed further in an attempt to resolve certain aspects that interest us in this chapter; these aspects mark a point of departure with respect to specific African cultural groups and their respective traditions.

From the moment they are pulled out of the universe of their "being"—that is, the homeland cultural context—the rigidity of the laws, values, and patterns that regulate the way of life of a tradition become ephemeral. One reason for this is that they became divorced from the totality of cultural expression, and the cultural elements in general and the transplanted musical elements in particular start to gradually lose their identity and spiritual meaning. In the cases under study, the structure has been maintained at the expense of function.

If the crux of the definition of "tradition" requires, as expressed by Balandier, "the *conformity* to rules of socially prescribed conduct" and "the *accession* to the specific order of society and of the culture in question," then slaveholders did not produce favorable conditions for observing tradition, but rather stood in opposition to them. In the new society, committed to new sets of relations and counterparts, even the desire to continue to obey a cultural practice is possibly obfuscated. Here, the variety of cultural material from various traditions makes assimilation (continuity) of any trait or specific cultural practice without some degree of modification improbable, resulting in conformity to a new set of rules and a new mode of life. Other phenomena could be analyzed to reveal their impact on the enslaved African's conformity (less than that of their descendants) to his or her tradition of origin. Yet these phenomena show not only persistence and continuity, but evidence of the evolution of musical traits.

Balandier tells us, "The tradition sometimes operates within collective and individual consciences, and within constitutive relations of social life."[173] If this is so, there is a reason to believe that the nonconformity to rules of conduct prescribed by society is nothing but a formal manifestation of weakness resulting from an individual dissociated from his or her cosmos. That is, after enslavement, the deculturalized and depersonalized individual does not feel governed by tradition anymore. For him or her, the constituent elements of a culture will have another meaning and these cultural elements that persist in individual memory will be adapted to the defined culture by the members of the new society to ensure continuity. It is this weakness that, for us, confirms the existence of this type of mutation. Transatlantic slaving became a primary factor or an exponent of both "external causality," which disrupted the network of existing relationships in society, as well as "internal causality," since it affected the formal framework of the individual.

In the Congo, a similar process of depersonalization, which influences a person's core being in various societies, can be detected in the creation of urban musical styles expressed in economically exploitative societies in the nineteenth and twentieth centuries.[174] Among other cradles of modern music from the Congo, there is the Chemin de Fer du Congo (Congo Railway) founded in 1889 and uniting the capital, Kinshasa, with the port of Matadi and the Union Minière du Haut Katanga (Katanga High Mining Union founded in 1906). In 1966, under president Mobutu, the latter company changed its name to the Générale Carrière des Mines (GECAMINES). Within the worker camps, around which some of the main cities in the Congo possibly may have emerged, members of different societies lived together for a given period as set forth by their respective labor contracts.

In beginning the workers came only at one station at a time. The majority was single and remained in camp for only a few months, after which they were forced to go back to their respective societies of origin. But by 1928, according to a "stabilization policy" adopted by company recruiters, married men hired could then be accompanied by their families to the labor camps, where they lived for at least three years, on a renewable basis. It can be inferred that the contractors per season could not have lost much of their respective cultures, because the interruption was very small and the period during which they lived together with others did not allow for intercultural or inter-ethnic acculturation to occur. This created a new, homogenized society from which would grow a lifestyle, means of artistic expression, etc., having as their basis the product of "ethnic" fusion on which the sociocultural, political, economic, and religious consensus of the new society would exert their forces in the shaping of new social patterns. In other words, the continuous contact for three years at the camp represents a relevant phenomenon that weakened their cultural activities and affected the constituent cultural members. This period can be seen as an important factor in making the individual memory ephemeral and encouraging a reluctance to maintain cultural patterns and values discussed above. It would not be a mistake to think of this same period as a kind of "rupture" for the individual and his or her culture, although this phenomenon is a voluntary migration, as opposed to forced transatlantic migration or transatlantic slaving.

The recruitment policy used by the companies to meet the demand for labor reveals several other phenomena that also led to an accelerated deculturalization or "detribalization" process. The recruitment policy did not have any "ethnic" or national boundaries. R. Cornevin cites M. Philipson, president of the Estrada de Ferro do Kongo, and writes, "Under these conditions, the recruitment from the west African coast, where black returnees had fear, have become difficult: It was necessary to hire black workers from the West Indies, Macau, and Chinese who didn't resist working under the Congo climate."[175] For GECAMINES, the labor problem persisted long after its first year of production (1913) and to cure this discrepancy, the workers were also employed outside the borders of the Congo: "The issue of manpower was always a cause of serious concern. In early 1913, the situation was still critical and certain jobs were paralyzed. Fortunately we had workers from Mozambique and Nyasaland." Later, the same source says, since "the beginning of its existence and for some years, the Union Minière still takes advantage of the organization established by Tanganyika and employs workers who are allowed to come to Zimbabwe...So, from 1920 to 1925, on average, half of the workers in Union Minière were foreigners—approximately 6,500 in 1925 out of the total of about 14,000 men."[176]

The acceleration of the "detribalization" process can also be seen in the distribution of housing inside the camp. According to S. Alexandre-Pyre, "In colonial times, the cultural factor was ignored. The economic needs were only cream for the workforce."[177] Although the cultural or "ethnic" displacement process in these labor camps in the Congo cannot be compared to that of enslaved Africans in Brazil, it would be wrong to believe that the principle of divide and conquer was based on the employer's fear of rebellion.

An analysis of the historical evolution of the modern music of Congo reveals that it emerged in the worker camps established in the 1940s.[178] More than a decade, this is the period during which the group had absorbed a cultural inventory and from different cultures selected their common denominators, and elements assimilated from the stronger or more influential culture came to constitute their new culture. The main musical compositions belonging to this period until end of the 1950s reveals that in this mixture of societies the time division of sixteen pulses predominated, particularly in the repertoire of composers from the Kasai region, notably Kasongo (Antoine) and Mwenda wa Bayeke (see transcript of Masanga).

One may wonder about the prevalence of this time division of sixteen pulses, which does not belong to the set of common denominators among the amalgamated societies noted above. This prevalence boils down to the large number of carriers of this musical element in the Kasai region.[179] We find the predominance of time line pattern of sixteen pulses both in the popular musical expressions of Brazil and the Congo. In the Congo, regional composers practice the incorporation of the pattern where it is believed to have originated. In other words, these composers learnt the rhythmic pattern in the worker camps, but are themselves bearers of cultural elements. In Brazil, the same pattern is found in *samba* not only in the second half of the nineteenth century, during which enslaved Africans carried out their secret activities between the Bantu regions and Brazil, but it appeared for the first time in Brazilian popular expression in the regions with large concentrations of enslaved Bantu peoples and their descendants.

Regardless of the nature of the depersonalization process resulting from colonization and enslavement, both of which essentially deprived the individual of his or her cosmos and resulting identity and existence. Crucial elements in musical expression prevailed in Bantu Africa and in Brail; these musical elements, whose traditional values (among societies in the Congo Basin) are important expressions of ritual and religious convictions, have become popular elements in Brazil. But a crisis in the individual core or collective Bantu consciousness must have occurred, thus affecting the carriers of these elements at the conceptual level. The transformations that affect one element or another do not have equal effect on all them, although the constituent elements of a society are in specific relations of interdependence and determination, a cultural element can either resist or yield to foreign cultural infiltration or domination.[180]

In this case study, the same observation can be made in relation to Bantu musical elements in Brazilian popular music. In addition to the metal double bell (*agogô*), which has similarities in its ritual and profane usage in black Africa and in Brazilian society, the friction drum (*cuíca*), the musical bow (*berimbau*), the basket rattle (*caxixi*) and the four-pulse rhythmic pattern were all part of a conceptual mutation. In Brazil, the organological structure of Bantu musical elements was maintained, and Europe's style of Christmas festivities and carnival manifestations were adopted.

We assume the total traditional ritual expression is analogous to the social structure, and view the constituent elements (dance, music, props, location, celebrant, rites, etc.) as part of a network of interdependent relationships. We can consider the rhythmic time divisions, the musical bow, the friction drum and the basket rattle as raw materials used to express the totality of their ritual expression. Each element represents an entity in which there is also another set of relationships between the component parts, either organological (in the case of musical instruments) or motif (in reference to rhythmic patterns). Not only are the constituent elements of ritual expression exposed to changes (resulting from identity loss), but all their component parts are also affected by the source of the changes. This explains why, in the course of industrialization of the *cuíca* or in the mass production of the *berimbau*, there have been various replacements of parts (e.g., leather used in the drum and rod, type of wood used).

In the Bantu philosophical conception, one can draw an imaginary cultural line between two antipodal states of being, going from "not" to "is." This is one cultural line that Kagame referred to as "existential movement," belonging to each particular element. On the other hand, Bantu philosophy has a clear distinction between the "is" and the "existing," although the relation between them is a functional relation. The "is" represents the material within this philosophy, the tangible aspect of an element or cultural member. According to the Bantu, for this structure to have palpable existence, it needs to "belong," creating thus an entity with other cultural elements of the same or different nature. Existence, in this sense, is a set of meanings (i.e., symbolic values) traditionally assigned to any cultural trace (i.e., member) inside a given set of cultural or "ethnic" relations. The being exists when within the totality of his cosmos. At the time of crisis, the being loses its existence (i.e., its meaning) in relation to the primary cosmos, and assumes another existence when inside a new cosmic core. In the Bantu conception, there has been a symbolic death of being in relation to the tradition, in relation with the society. One can even interpret this as a spiritual death and not physical, affecting the function (a set value) and not the structure (that which "is").

In light of this philosophical concept, several similarities become evident. For example, the directional movement of the cultural imaginary line evolves in a direction opposite to that expressed by Kagame as existential movement. The cultural elements (such as their carriers) begin with a full identity (existence), i.e., the being and all the traditionally assigned values. At the other extreme, there is the state of non-being in Bantu terms. With the break from their respective cosmos (a phenomenon resulting from enslavement), each element starts its movement along the imaginary line in the direction of the non-being; and along that line, whose distance can be measured in time, he begins to be what he was. At the end of the non-being (symbolizing a condition to be performed), the presence of cultural elements transplanted to the new society should be seen as a manifestation of their persistence. Their continuity provide evidence of their assimilation into the new expression; and the evolution would not be the transplanted elements, but the old "is" assumes a more new existence.

Our argument extends the analogy of the relationship of "is" and "life" to "structure" and "function." Just as the *muntu* "is" exists only in relation to its vital values traditionally found in the cosmos, structuralist social scientists tell us that the structure is only observable in operation.[181] In both cases, the relationship of functional interdependence emphasizes its reason for being. In short, the mutation in these Bantu conceptual and musical elements implies continuity and a rupture as experienced by their carriers to the Americas. By means of their carriers' collective memory, these musical elements survived the collapse of their respective cosmoses. It is from these same memories affected by new phenomena that they were played in the new society, thus assuming a new existence to ensure their continuity.

A good example of rupture can be seen in the "nonexisting line" of each Bantu musical element uncovered. The rupture, which affects the identity of each element by depriving it of its cosmos, originates in a new and totally different form at the end of nonexistence, as conceived by cultural carriers. This end, which becomes nonexistent in relation to the original being, becomes "existing" again by assuming new identity as part of a new cosmos in which it is assimilated. Some of the original traits remain; and so begins a new line of being or nonexistence. All are not only for reasons of persistence and continuity, whose cradle is either individual or collective memory. As a phenomenon, the rupture is not in itself an action but results from an action; it is precisely for this reason that its operational base lies not in material forms but at the conceptual core. Each severance generates a rupture that occurs simultaneously but affects two levels of different considerations: the physical and the conceptual.

Transatlantic slaving led to the transplantation of African societies, languages, traditions, etc. to the Americas with completely different cultures, governed by a new network of power relationships. In essence, there was a severance and the creation of two realities and structures. This severance is also seen in the case of musical instruments, originating in their Bantu cultural and ritual contexts and relocated to Brazil, where their use became profane. At the same time, due to the forced divorce of Bantu cultural members from their respective cosmos, a rupture occurred. This is the time during which the process of depersonalization and loss of identity began to operate in the formal, conceptual core of the individual. This process (nonexistence line or conceptual shift) works as a filter, blocking the function and permeating the structure of cultural elements. These elements, retained in the collective memory, will be played according to the rules of the new society—thus forming a basis for modification—while other elements will not be playable due to the loss of its identity and related values, which are the substance of the cosmos to which they belong.

A similar situation is found in the colonization process. The exodus from villages to industrialized centers also represented two levels of structural realities: one governed by a given tradition and one whose values and norms are acculturated. A behavior deemed tolerable can be considered unconventional in another context due to its nature. Therefore, the process of colonization can certainly be placed under the theme of severance. In the deculturalization or "detribalization" process, there were some structural habits arising from "ethnic" centers but with newly assigned values different from those who had them in their respective tradition. The change in attributive values resulted from a conditioning of the core where the values are designed.

A mutation takes place—in the vocabulary of the social sciences—only when considered in addition to the concept of time. If mutation is a synonym of rupture, it should be defined as a conceptual conditioning resulting from a crisis, and the consequence of a series of changes affecting a society in a new way. Accepting that society is composed of individuals that define a set of relations (e.g., norms, values, etc.) by which the individual's behavior is governed, this conditioning occurs at the individual's formal level, at which he or she designs the network of relationships that are the foundation of society in one lives. In other words, mutation has been used in this study as the conceptual shift that begins with a traditional or indigenous cosmic reality break and ends with the beginning of a new cosmic entity in a new culture—a state of mind that exists between being and non-being.

CHAPTER 5

PERSISTENCE AND CONTINUITY OF BANTU MUSICAL ELEMENTS IN BRAZIL

One of the objects treated in the previous chapter was the semantics of the adopted term "mutation," giving it a new dimension beyond that which it has in the social sciences. The chapter demonstrated that mutation is not a change in itself, but mainly a phenomenon resulting from an act that can cause rupture at the individual's conceptual level, and where the subsequent changes are designed for the first time. The present chapter is dedicated to other phenomena, focusing particularly on the same Bantu musical elements. These phenomena are associated with the terms "persistence" and "continuity," in the sense of pure change or evolution of social structures and cultural traits. A closer examination of their semantics reveals, in a broad sense, an interconnected relationship that deserves greater attention.

Persistence is not necessarily continuity, although the former constitutes a condition *sine qua non* for the latter, and occupies a prime position if we consider both in chronological order. In other words, persistence ensures continuity. Henry Pratt Fairchild discusses "social continuity" as the persistence of social groups, of their interaction, customs, traditions, and beliefs, and emphasizes that persistence is at the core of continuity.[182]

In his studies of cultural contact and acculturation, Herskovits emphasized in his theory of "reinterpretation" the retention of an African psyche that could accept traces of Western culture but think about them and live them in an African way. In his book *The Myth of the Negro Past*, Herskovits summarized his methodological approach in these terms: "In terms of this approach, the research turned not to the issue of which Africanisms were transported in unchanged form, but instead how cultural accommodation and integration have been achieved by contact of Africans with Europeans and American Indians."[183] For Bastide,

"The problem...is to understand how so many Africans cultural traits could not resist the juggernaut servile regime."[184]

For the carriers of Bantu musical elements to overcome the process of depersonalization, these elements had to have had deep values assigned to them by their bearers, and the primary values were linked, where appropriate, to other values that emerge from the new environment. The first part of our discussion will be concerned with this persistence of Bantu musical elements in the mind of their carriers before their adaptation and assimilation in new societies. The second part, which focuses on continuity, uses sociological theories in general and approaches to cultural contact in particular.

Starting from the premise that the philosophical principle of existence (*muntu*) is the core of Bantu identity, the major reason for the persistence of certain musical elements would be found in the metamorphosis from a "nonexistent" state to a "being" state. This Bantu philosophical principle, as described by Tempels, forms a vertical hierarchical structure that coordinates the network of relations between the constituent elements, and establishes the "traditional order" of the world for the *muntu*.[185] On top of this structure, there is a Supreme Being or Creator from which emanates the dynamic vital force that animates the universe. The ancestors occupy the second level; they are the first into whom the Creator breathed life. They are also the founders of the societies and clans, protected and governed through local leadership. In the world of the dead, the deceased are immediate family members who have become ancestors with the appropriate ceremony. In the world of the living, a remarkable vertical hierarchy begins with the societal leaders who act as intermediaries between their subjects and the ancestors. These leaders govern in accordance with the laws and the wisdom of the past encapsulated in tradition. One can draw a parallel between the hierarchical structures of the animal world and the world of humans. The lion, for example, is often considered a symbol of the authority of the village or societal leader. This is true among the Luba, the Kongo, the Kuba, and other societies of the Congo Basin. The last two levels in hierarchical scale are occupied, respectively, by the vegetable and mineral worlds, in which a similar hierarchy can also be found.[186]

The hierarchical principle is found in all constitutive facets in the world of the *muntu*. At the societal level, the hierarchical structure defines, through performed functions, criteria that can be classified as a division of labor along traditional lines. J. Cuvelier pointed this out among the Bakongo, where one leader named Nsaku ne Vunda of the Lau clan, who is believed to be the grandfather of Kingdom of Kongo's founder, played the role of intermediary between the living and the ancestors. "And as we know," writes Cuvelier, "that for every king that should reign, Nsaku ne Vunda must be present. If he is not present, his authority cannot be recognized."[187] After all, this spiritual responsibility also contributes to the authority of the Lau clan: "This combination of two powers, expressed solemnly during changes of reign, is sealed by the mandatory marriage of the sovereign of Kongo with a girl belonging to the clan leader of Nsaku's lineage. It is expressed by a politically prominent position of two representatives of the latter to court of Kongo, by a special status in the Mbata province where clan members reside and where this clan governs the Nsaku Lau people."[188] This division of power and labor, as defined by a hierarchical structure, can also be seen on a smaller scale in which family structures are distinguished by the inherited, hierarchical and earned responsibilities.[189]

Elsewhere, we have provided an extensive description of cultural behaviors among the Bantu in Congo, revealing their structural influence on the song's design. This influence is reflected in songs of praise and belongs to a set of rules whose purpose is to maintain the proper relationship between the constituent nodes of the network. This is confirmed by the many respectful ways parents treat their children and children treat their parents, each one emphasizing the existing hierarchical order.[190] If these codes of behavior are fundamentally regarded as a trait or habit, or, if they have transformed it, it is because they belong to the whole of traditional organization.

In the visual arts, the traditional criteria for a division of labor also reinforce the hierarchical order under consideration. For a considerable time, the arts were functionally practiced in African communities, and what is more interesting is the fact that art was not practiced by anyone; it was reserved for special members of the community who were believed to have learned the craft of spirits and not of mortals. For this reason, the practice of art is restricted to certain families in particular, despite changes over the generations. E. V. de Oliveira expressed this fact in following terms: "The traditional sculptor generally is a professional male belonging to certain groups, a specialized craftsman, the only one in the village who sometimes knows the virtues and significance of trees he uses or the animals he represents. Among the Bakuba, the sculptors belong to a distinct class and its delegate has primacy in the court."[191]

With regards to musical instruments, particularly membranophone, idiophone (e.g., xylophone), and aerophone (e.g., flute) instruments, we find a similar situation. In Gabon and among the Luba in the Congo, such instruments are made by community artisans, who, it is believed, the ancestors of the society bequeathed the "king's note" or the "mother's note," to which all the instruments have to be tuned. Once again, it is quite remarkable that this knowledge is a legacy from generation to generation within the same lineage, and also serves as a criterion for the division of labor among community members and situates the hierarchical relationship between them. This is revealed by the status acquired by the individual who performs out these functions within the community.

The hierarchical structure is also found in a set of musical instruments and in some other musical rudiments (harmony, rhythmic patterns, etc.), characterizing a given musical culture. This is true for the majority of African societies—in Rwanda, Ghana, and the Kuba region, to mention few—in which sets of drums constitute the symbol of the king's supremacy in the court. Among the Asante, a new set of *atumpam* is made for every new king and presented to him during his installation. For the Kuba, the drum set is not for the individual but for the throne. The original set of Kuba royal drums, dating from the seventeenth century remains in the Institut de Musées Nationaux in Kinshasa since 1973, while a replica lies in the Musée royal de l'Afrique centrale in Tervuren (Brussels). Usually, maong the Luba, similar drums are only carried out by a person connected to the court for personal dances like the *mpundu*.

It is often found that from the moment in which a musical instrument, a dance step, or a rhythmic pattern was assigned to a given ceremony or to a particular dignitary, they become an integral part of the ritual and are never used for another event or purpose. Therefore, we can believe that (1) there is a hierarchical relationship or a vertical structure among the constituents of the various facets of African societies. Among the Bantu, this hierarchy is best understood when combined with the principle of belonging, which in turn is based on the identity of the *muntu*; (2) seen from this perspective, each one of the elements discussed above can certainly be regarded as belonging to the nucleus of existence of the individual or the ritual to which they are assigned and which constitutes a "cosmos."

Some may wonder if it is appropriate to consider the survival of musical elements in the memory of enslaved Bantu peoples because those elements belonged to the set of cultural habits or coded behaviors, or because they were an integral part of the individual's Bantu life. Without repeating the role played by each Bantu musical element discussed in earlier chapters, it is important to summarize here in order to highlight the congruency between the cases illustrated above and the musical materials. Generally, with the exception of the double bell with no clapper, which has a role in most musical sets, we revealed the traditionally assigned value for each of the other musical instruments and rhythmic patterns that define their respective roles in various functional societies. The cosmic identity in context of the Bantu philosophy was underpinned by what we have referred to as the principle of belonging. In short, these musical elements did not escape the gravity of hierarchical relationships or the nucleus of existence as found in their source societies.

In light of the evidence, it can be argued the idea of belonging for the individual—which is central to the nucleus of existence—is the main reason and *ipso facto* phenomenon for its retention in the memory of the individual. It is this Bantu nucleus of existence that survived the rupture and and that supported the crystallization of cultural elements within the individual memory, and which, when combined with the set of social factors, became important in the preservation and continuity of cultural elements within a new society.

Up until now, some might think we have adopted a functionalist approach, such as that applied by Herskovits, to the problems concerning the survival of "Africanisms" outside their continent of origin. "If whole sections of culture remain," wrote Herskovits, "despite the terrible crushing of slavery, it is because African customs served something or was useful, exercising an essential function for the survival of the black group."[192] But could we compare the indispensable role of survival as articulated by Herskovits, to what we have referred to as the Bantu nucleus of existence? While Herskovits saw the problem in broader perspectives, we have narrowed the scope of the problem to individuals. Viewed from this perspective, the persistence of Bantu musical elements in the memory of their carriers, in spite of cultural disruption and its continuity in time and space, depends neither on the constitution of the collective memory of the carriers nor on their frameworks of social memory, as Halbwachs argued.[193]

In the analytical discussion around each musical element, several issues related to their respective persistence and continuity become evident. In general, these issues can be identified as follows: the physical and temporal space that separates the cultural carriers from their cultural cradles; and then the common denominator of such elements, both among the various societies or regional clusters (e.g., Bantu, Sudanese) and those of Bantu origin. With respect to historical time, one can doubt the survival of Bantu musical elements, since there is time gap between the arrival of first enslaved Bantu people in the last half of sixteenth century and the moment when these elements appeared in Brazilian popular expression at the beginning of the twentieth century. In this gap, many generations have sprang from forced miscegenation, not only between enslaved Africans from various societies and ecologies but also between the whites and their enslaved Africans, including miscegenation between Africans and Amerindians. Stressing one reason for the obliteration of cultural boundaries between Africans and the ephemeralization of their tradition in the course of generational change, Bastide wrote, "the cultural recruiting ceased; even more, the marriages were between different cultural groups and the children born of such unions were Créole with no resumption of a particular tradition."[194]

It tends to be taken for granted that the *samba* form was created in regions where, historically, there was a strong concentration of enslaved Bantu peoples and where the time divisions of four and sixteen pulses in *samba* predominated. In consideration of the strong diffusion of *samba*'s predecessor, *samba de umbigada*, which can be considered a common denominator among the enslaved Africans due to their common characteristics, Edison Carneiro and Rafael de Menezes Bastos have also demonstrated that the so-called "samba zone" coincides with regions where agriculture was the main economic activity. The illegal trafficking of enslaved Africans to Brazil, which invigorated and strengthened Bantu cultural practices with new elements, must be taken into account. Illegal trafficking occurred, among other places, in the Rio de Janeiro region, where the time division of sixteen pulses would have been introduced in *samba*, and thus characterized the so-called *samba carioca*. Viewed from this perspective, this musical or cultural pattern must have been a common denominator among enslaved Africans, becoming a part of their cultural inventory and thus creating a basis for new expressions in the region. As for the time division of four pulses, it becomes even more complex since this pattern seems to have been popular well before the possible date of creation for *samba*.

Similar observations can also be made about the *berimbau*, with respect to the time of its integration with *capoeira*. Although the bow and arrow are known as hunting tools in most African societies, an adaptation of the bow to musical expression was noticed mainly among the Bantu of Angola, where the popularity of the instrument was an important part of the repertoire.[195] The basket rattle (*caxixi*) presents a similar situation. A pertinent question, however, arises: Was this instrument included in the *capoeira* set simultaneously with the *berimbau*, an instrument with which it is currently associated in Brazil? A review of the literature on the *berimbau* and the *caxixi* makes it clear that in their regions of origin they were not played together. Kubik discusses the *berimbau*—*mbulumbumba*—among the Kung in Angola, but nothing is mentioned that would indicate the combination of these two instruments in any musical ensemble. Through the Luba, the *caxixi* must have reached the seaside of west central Africa, and was then transported to Brazil. The more common musical bow—*lunkomba*—is not played with the basket rattle for the simple reason that they have to different uses—ceremonial or social functions. While the basket rattle is used in *bampamba* events, the *lunkomba* is more used in hunter societies and also played individually by traditional healers, to pass time during a solitary task.

These instruments were, in fact, the common denominators among the enslaved Africans in Brazil. The rhythmic patterns of four or sixteen pulses coincide with areas of concentration enslaved Bantu and their descendants, since the beginning of the nineteenth century, with the coffee culture of the Vale do Paraíba. It was in this region that the enslaved continued to practice certain musical forms such as the *lundu* and the popular old musical form known as *modinha*; it was also in the region that the latter won its supremacy in carioca *samba*. The vast concentration of enslaved Africans from Angola in Salvador (Bahia) certainly justifies why *capoeira* could only be created in this region and that the use of the *berimbau* had to spread therein. It can be argued the majority of these musical elements and forms with which they are associated in Brazil were, first, local-regional styles, which must have been common denominators among the locals.

Be that as it may, the forced displacement of African "ethnic" members by slaveholders and subsequent miscegenation suggests that prior to reaching a national homogeneity, even at the artistic level, this had already been achieved regionally and justified the existence of certain regional expressions. In music, the "creole drum" continues to characterize the Maranhense musical style, while the *baião* represents the northeastern musical style. Other regional characteristics are also found in various cultural practices. While Rio de Janeiro celebrates its carnival, practically the entire north and northeastern parts of Brazil emphasizes the festive equivalent of *bumba-meu-boi* and *maracatu*. In Fortaleza (in the state of Ceará), during the carnival period, there are groups of *maracatu* that participate in the parade and not the *samba* schools as in Rio de Janeiro. A similar situation is found in São Luís where the *bumba-meu-boi* is the largest carnival group that parades through the city. Gradually these and other regional old styles have made their presence known in other parts of the nation by means of internal migration—a vehicle of national cultural homogeneity. In addition to carioca *samba*, *bumba-meu-*

boi, and *capoeira*, other disseminated cultural expressions were taken for granted in consideration of national homogeneity. There is the *maculelê* whose dissemination may well go back to the internal migration from Bahia to Ceará and Minas Gerais. What are interesting are the name changes according local-regional mutation. The original name *maculelê* is known in the state of Ceará as the *manera-o-pau*, and with time, reached Minas Gerais (probably originating from Ceará) and became known as the *minera-o-pau*.

This exhaustive discussion emphasizes regional influences in cultural practices, which ultimately confirms that there was some sort of African "ethnic" concentration to justify the creation of certain Brazilian forms. The persistence of certain African cultural elements could only have been possible if these were common denominators among enslaved community members. For these musical elements to have reached commonplace status in their respective regions, homogeneity must have occurred in these localities, regardless of its intensity or the time required for the crystallization of cultural units.

One can very well establish a parallel between this study and what occurred in the creation of the Congo's modern music in the labor camps around the economically exploitative companies, such as the Chemin De Fer du Congo (Congo Railway) and the Union Miniére du Haut Katanga (Katanga High Mining Union). In the case of the latter, which was created in 1906, it was only in 1928, following the so-called stabilization policy (under which the company permitted married men to be accompanied by their families to the worker camps), that we can begin to think of cultural homogeneity in the camps. In the creation of African American musical expression, it was only in 1900 (281 years after the arrival of the first enslaved Africans in 1619) that the musical forms began to become mainstream. What is the reason for the chronological difference? Several studies have revealed the great cruelty of transatlantic slaving on African "ethnic" members in the United States as compared to Brazil. E. Franklin Frazier wrote:

> The African family system was destroyed
> and the slave was separated from relatives

and friends. In addition, in the United States, there was little chance that he could resume friendship and old associations. If by chance he found slavery companions with whom he could communicate in his native language, he was separated from them....Any memory that he could have retained of his native land and customs became insignificant in the Americas.[196]

Though Frazier's argument is not completely accurate, the separation he spoke about must have occurred in Brazil's plantations and not at the regional level, since the presence of African "ethnic" groups (called "nations") and activities such as the construction of churches certainly confirm this fact. In Salvador, as in Minas Gerais, the majority of the "nations" tried to remain as pure as possible, and for some, the amount of skin pigmentation had become the main criterion for admission of a new member.

The second part of this study presented a detailed discussion with relation to the organological structure of the friction drum and its uses, both among the Bantu societies in Congo and in some European countries (e.g., Spain, Portugal), although there is no satisfactory explanation of its origin. In Brazil, this instrument maintained the structure derived from the Bantu, while its functions remained of European origin. The acceptance of the structure by the ruling class can certainly be seen as a relevant factor to the continuity of the instrument in the new society. This practice is also common in other "Africanisms" in Brazil; among others, African religions, which have resisted over the course of centuries and of which there have been some syncretism that has acquired peculiar characteristics. On the other hand, we noticed that for a considerable time the *samba* and its authors were persecuted by the police; this happened until the early 1920s, as they were considered undesirable by members of the ruling class. A similar situation occurred with *capoeira*. But today, these are forms of cultural expressions hailed as part of the national Brazilian character. Why is this so?

Over a considerable period of time, the number of whites in *samba* schools has grown considerably. In recent decades, the board of directors for these schools has a white majority. In Bahia, as well as the whole nation, *capoeira* has been organized in academies and considered a form of national defense. Although some authors attribute the phenomenon to capitalism and socioeconomic reasons, the fact remains that the presence of whites in *samba* and *capoeira* has helped to stop the persecution and allowed us to establish these forms as expression of the national character, thus ensuring their continuity within Brazilian society.

On a carnival day, a professor Teófilo of the Department of Sociology at the University of São Paulo noted in an informal conversation that the structural nature of wards (*alas*) succession and highlights (*destaques*) of the *samba* school reflects the white (European) presence. The organization is characterized by positioning the *samba* school in a way that there is a decrease in the amount of skin pigmentation. In other words, the school starts with a white skin and ends with black skin. During a carnival in Rio de Janeiro, I noticed that virtually all the highlights of the main *samba* schools in the first group were white women, while the majority ward of Bahians, at end of the school, was composed of black women. Although this practice cannot articulate or does not prove any racial implication, it does not contradict this study's hypotheses.

CONCLUSION

Throughout this study, we made our arguments using extra-musical cultural aspects as a backdrop and to reveal the behavior of the carriers of cultural elements, inside and as outside their cultural origin. Here, our aim is to simply summarize main points presented in previous chapters.

We argued in this case study that Bantu musical rudiments and instruments survived in Brazilian culture and popular artistic expression. The enslaved Bantu peoples which came to Brazil were composed of cultural or "ethnic" member constituents of the first Kingdom of Kongo, which reached its apogee in the sixteenth century, and of the second kingdom, which emerged after the displacement of the first and was permeated by migrants who came from the interior regions of the Congo Basin. The cultural interactions in the past occurred in periods prior to transatlantic slaving activities were carried out by the Portuguese and Dutch empires in the Bantu coastal regions of west central Africa, allowing for the formation of a cultural unity between the aforementioned kingdoms and the rest of the basin. That unity was underpinned by the "common cultural denominators" shared by their carriers.

But the effect of those slaving activities left a significant mark on the African carriers of Bantu musical elements, and also caused great repercussions in the history of Africa and the Americas. Once separated from a whole cultural context, the musical elements are subjected to a mutation of their "traditional" Bantu design to the "popular" Brazilian design, sacrificing their functions to maintain their structures in the Americas.

On other hand, the persistence of these elements in the memory of their carriers was demonstrated in psychological terms, which, as a constituent of the Bantu cosmos, defined the *muntu*'s identity and the musical elements vital to its existence. In other words, if the musical elements persisted in Bantu memory, it is because they were functional. In Brazil, the conceptual mutation was a form of adaptation of musical elements in the style of the new society, gaining a new existence that ensured its continuity in an deculturalizing and dehumanizing re-socialization process.

BIBLIOGRAPHY

Alexandre-Pyre, Sybille. "L'origine de la population du centre urbain de Lubumbashi," in, *Publications de l'Université Officielle du Congo à Lubumbashi* 19 (1969): 141-150.

Almeida, Renato. *História da música brasileira*. 2ª ed. Rio de Janeiro: F. Briguiet & Compania, 1942.

_____. *Música folclórica e música popular*. Rio de Janeiro: Instituto Brasileiro de Educação, Ciência e Cultura, Comissão Nacional de Folclore, 1958.

_____. "A influência da música negra no Brasil," in, *Colóquio sobre as relações entre países da América Latina e da África*. Rio de Janeiro: UNESCO/IBECC, September 24-30, 1963.

Alvarenga, Oneyda. "A influência negra na música brasileira." *Boletim Latino Americano da Música* 6, 6 (abril, 1946): 357-408.

_____. *Música popular brasileira*. São Paulo: Globo, 1950.

Amaral, Braz Hermenegildo do. "Os grandes mercados de escravos africanos: as tribos importadas, sua distribuição regional." *Annaes do Congresso Internacional de História da América,* realizado pelo Instituto Histórico e Geográfico Brasileiro em setembro de 1922 Rio de Janeiro. Rio de Janeiro: Imprensa Nacional, 1927, pp. 435-496

Andrade, Mário de. "Origens das danças dramáticas brasileiras." *Revista Brasileira de Música* 2, 1 (1935): 34-39.

_____. "Os Congos." *Boletín Latino Americano de Música* 1, 1 (1935): 57-70.

_____. "O samba rural paulista." *Revista do Arquivo Municipal* 4, 41 (1937): 37-116.

_____. "Cândido Inácio da Silva e o lundu." *Revista Brasileira de Música* 10, (1944): 17-39.

_____. "As danças dramáticas do Brasil." *Boletín Latino Americano de Música* 6, 6 (1946): 49-78.

_____. *Ensaio sobre música brasileira*. São Paulo: Martins, 1968.

Andrade, Nair de. "Musicalidade do escravo negro no Brasil." *Novos Estudos Afro-Brasileiros*. Rio de Janeiro: Civilização Brasileira, 1937, pp. 192-200.

Araújo, Alceu Maynard. *Cultura popular brasileira*. São Paulo: Melhoramentos, 1973.

Araújo, Mozart de. *A modinha e o lundu no século XVIII*. São Paulo: Ricordi, 1963.

Azevedo, Luis Heitor Correia de. "Música popular nordestina." *Cultura Política* 4, 40 (1944): 233-236.

_____. "Música negra do Nordeste." *Cultura Política* 5, 48 (1945): 18-36.

Balandier, Georges. *La vie quotidienne au royaume de Kongo du XVI au XVIII siécle*. Paris: Hachette, 1965.

_____. (ed.). *Sociologie des mutations*. Paris: Anthropos, 1970.

_____. *Sens et puissance*. Paris: Presses Universitaires de France, 1971.

_____. *Anthropos-Logiques*. Paris: Presses Universitaires de France, 1974.

Barroso, Sebastião M. "Música e cultura." *Mensário do Jornal do Comércio* 9, 2 (1940): 275-279.

Bascom, William Russell & Herskovits, Melville J. *Continuity and Change in African cultures*. Chicago: University of Chicago Press, 1959.

Bastide, Roger. "Le batuque de Porto-Alegre." *Acculturation in the Americas. Proceedings and Selected Papers of the XXIXth International Congress of Americanists*, 1952, pp. 195-206.

_____. "Le principe de coupure et le comportement afro-brésilien." *Anaïs do XXXI Congresso Internacional de Americanistas* 1, (1954): 493-503.

_____. "La causalité externe et la causalité interne dans l'explication sociologique." *Cahiers Internationaux de Sociologie* 21, (1956): 77-99.

_____. *Les religions africaines au Brésil*. Paris: Presses Universitaires de France, 1960.

_____. (ed.). *Sens et usages du terme structure dans les sciences humaines et sociales*. Paris: Mouton, 1962.

_____. *Les Amériques noires*. Paris: Payot, 1967.

_____. *Le prochain et le lointain*. Paris: Cujas, 1970.

Bastos, Rafael J. de Menezes. "Las músicas tradicionales del Brasil" *Revista Musical Chilena 28*, 125 (1974): 21-77.

Bebey, Francis. *Musique de l'Afrique*. Paris: Horizons de France, 1969.

Béhague, Gérard. "The Lundu and the Modinha of Brazil in the 19th Century." *Symposium of the College Music Society 7* (1967): 103-106.

_____. "Biblioteca da Ajuda (Lisboa) Mss 1595/1596: Two Eighteenth-Century Anonymous Collections of Modinhas." *Yearbook of the Inter-American Institute for Musical Research IV* (1968): 44-81.

_____. (ed.). *Music and Black Ethnicity: The Caribbean and South America*. New Brunswick: Transaction Publishers, 1994.

Berardinelli, Cleonice. *Auto de Vicente Anes Joeira*, 2ª ed. Guanabara: Instituto Nacional do Livro, 1963.

Bergson, Henri. *Matière et Mémoire*, 92ª ed. Paris: Presses Universitaires de France, 1968.

Bethell, Leslie. *A Abolição do Tráfico de Escravos no Brasil*. São Paulo: Editora da Universidade de São Paulo, 1976.

Birmingham, David. *A conquista portuguesa de Angola*. Porto: A Regra do Jogo, 1965.

_____. "The Date and Significations of the Imbangala Invasion of Angola." *Journal of African History 6*, 2 (1965): 143-152.

Boxer, Charles Ralph. *Salvador de Sá e a luta pelo Brasil e Angola 1602-1686*. São Paulo: Editora da Universidade de São Paulo, 1973.

Braga, Ernani. "Toadas de Xangô do Recife: estudos afro-brasileiros." *I Congresso Afro-Brasileiro Reunido no Recife em 1934*. Vol. 1 (1935): 265-268.

Brandel, Rose. *The Music of Central Africa*. The Hague: Martinus Nijhoff, 1961.

Cabral, Sérgio. *As escolas de samba: o quê, quem, como, quando e por quê*. Rio de Janeiro: Fontana, 1974.

Campos, Augusto de. *Balanço da bossa e outras bossas*. São Paulo: Perspectiva, 1974.

Cardim, Fernão. *Tratado da terra e da gente do Brasil*. São Paulo: Companhia Editora Nacional, 1939.

Carneiro, Edison. *Religiões negras: notas de etnografia religiosa*. Rio de Janeiro: Civilização Brasileira, 1936.

_____. *Negros Bantus*. Rio de Janeiro: Civilização Brasileira, 1937.

_____. "Structure of African Cults in Bahia." *Journal of American Folklore* 53 (1940): 271-278.

_____. *Antologia do negro brasileiro*. São Paulo: Globo, 1950.

_____. *Samba de umbigada*. Rio de Janeiro: Ministério da Educação e Cultura, 1961.

_____. *Carta do samba*. Rio de Janeiro: Ministério da Educação e Cultura, 1962.

_____. *O quilombo dos Palmares*. Rio de Janeiro: Civilização Brasileira, 1966.

_____. "Cultos africanos no Brasil." In: *Planeta 1* (1972): 48-59.

Carvalho, Henrique Augusto Dias de. *Ethnographia e história tradicional dos povos da Lunda*. Lisboa: Imprensa Nacional, 1890.

Cascudo, Luis da Câmara. "Instrumentos musicais dos negros no norte do Brasil." *Movimento Brasileiro* 1, 3 (1929): 9.

_____. *Dicionário do folclore brasileiro*. 3rd ed. Brasília: Instituto Nacional do Livro, Ministério da Educação e Cultura, 1972.

Cavazzi, Giovanni Antonio. *Istorica Descrizione de' Trè Regni Congo, Matamba, et Angola*. Bologna: Giacomo Monti, 1687.

Chamberlain, Henry, Lieutenant. *Views and Costumes of the City and Neighborhood of Rio de Janeiro, Brazil*. London: Colombian Press, 1822.

Chase, Gilbert. *A Guide to the Music of Latin America*. Washington: Library of Congress and Pan American Union, 1962.

Clark, F. Desmond. "African Prehistory: Opportunities for Collaboration Between Archaeologists, Ethnographers and Linguists," in *Language and History in Africa* edited by David Dalby. London: Frank Cass and Company, 1970, pp. 1-19.

Clayton, Martin et al. *The Cultural Study of Music: A Critical Introduction.* New York: Routledge, 2003.

Clifton, James A. *Introduction to cultural anthropology: Essays in the Scope and Methods of the Science of Man.* Boston: Houghton Mifflin, 1968.

Colle, Révérend Père. *Les Baluba (Congo Belge): sociologie descriptive, Tome 2,* Bruxelles: A. Dewit, 1913.

Compan, Charles. *Dictionnaire de danse.* Paris: Cailleau, 1787.

Cornet, René Jules. *Maniema: le pays de mangeurs d'hommes.* Bruxelles: Cuypers, 1955.

_____. *Art de l'Afrique noire, au pays du fleuve Zaire.* Bruxelas, 1972.

Cornevin, Robert & Marianne. *Histoire de l'Afrique, des origines à nos jours.* Paris: Payot, 1956.

_____. *Histoire de l'Afrique dès origines à la deuxième guerre mondiale.* Paris : Payot, 1964.

Cornevin, Robert. *Le Zaire, ex-Congo-Kinshaa.* Paris: Presses Universitaires de France, 1972.

Costa, E. Viotti da. *Da senzala à colônia.* São Paulo: Difusão Européia do Livro, 1966.

Costa, Pereira da. "Rei do Congo." *Journal do Brasil,* 21/04/1901.

Dart, Raymond A. "Racial Origins," in, *Bantu-Speaking Tribes of South Africa: An Etehnographical Survey.* 6ª ed., Edited for the (South African) Inter-University Committee for African Studies by Isaac Shapera. London: Routledge & Kegan Paul, 1959, pp. 1-31.

Debret, Jean-Baptiste. *Voyage pittoresque et historique au Brésil, ou séjour d'un artiste français au Brésil depuis 1816 jusqu'en 1831 inclusivement.* 3 vols. Paris: Firmin Didot Frères, 1834-1839.

De Jonghe, Edouard & Vanhove, Julien. *Les formes d'asservissement dans les sociétés indigènes du Congo-Belge.* Bruxelles, 1949.

Delachaux, Théodore & Thiébaud, Charles-E. *Pays et peuples d'Angola.* Neuchâtel : Editions Victor Attinger, 1934.

Deschamps, Hubert. *Histoire générale de l'Afrique noire: des origines à nos jours*, 2 vols. Paris: Presses Universitaires de France, 1970.

Dias, Jorge. *Escultura africana no museu de etnologia do ultramar*. Lisboa: Junta de Investigação do Ultramar, 1968.

Diop, Cheikh Anta. *Nations nègres et culture*. Paris: Editions Africaines, 1954.

_____. *The African Origin of Civilization: Myth or Reality*. New York: Lawrence Hill, 1974.

Duprat, Régis & Orbino, Nise P. "O estanco da música no Brasil colonial." *Yearbook of the Inter-American Institute for Musical Research 4* (1968): 98-109.

Duvignaud, Jean. *Durkheim: Sa Vie, Son Oeuvre, avec un Exposé de sa Philosophie*. Paris: Presses Universitaires de France, 1965

Ehret, Christopher. "Patterns of Bantu and Central Sudanic Settlement in Central and

Southern Africa (ca. 1000 BC-500 AD)." *Transafrican Journal of History 3* (1969): 1-71.

_____. "Bantu Origins and History: Critique and Interpretation." *Transafrican Journal of History 2* (1972): 1-9.

_____. "Cattle-keeping and Milking in Eastern nd Southern African History: The Linguistic Evidence." *Journal of Africn History*, VIII, I, 1967, pp. 1-17.

Expilly, Charles. *La traite, l'émigration et la colonisation au Brésil*. Paris : A. Lacroix, Verboeckhoven et Cie, 1865.

Fagg, William. *Sculptures Africaines: les univers artistique des tribus d'Afrique noire*. Paris: F. Harzan, c. 1965.

Fairchild, Henry Pratt (ed.). *Diccionario de sociología*. México: Fundo de Cultura Económica, 1949.

Fernandes, Florestan. "Congada e batuques em Sorocaba." *Sociologia* 5, 2 (1943): 242-246.

Ferraz, Aydano do Couto. "Volta à África." *Revista do Arquivo Municipal de São Paulo 54* (1939): 175-178.

Ferreira, Alexandre Rodrigues. *Viagem filosófica pelas capitanias do Grão Para, Rio Negro, Mato Grosso e Cuiabá, 1783-1792.* Rio de Janeiro: Conselho Federal de Cultura, 1971.

Ferretti, Sérgio Figueiredo (Ed.). *Tambor de Crioula: Ritual e Espetáculo.* São Luís: Serviço de Imprensa e Obras Gráficos do Estado, 1978.

Fetterman, David M. *Ethnography: Step-by-Step.* Third Edition. Los Angeles: Sages, 2010.

Filho, Dornas J. "A influência social do negro brasileiro." *Revista do Arquivo Municipal de São Paulo* 5, 51 (1938): 97-134.

_____. *A escravidão no Brasil.* Rio de Janeiro, 1939.

Filho, Luiz Vianna. *O negro na Bahia.* São Paulo: Livraria José Olympio, 1946.

Freyre, Gilberto. *Casa-grande e senzala.* 16ª ed. Rio de Janeiro: Livraria José Olýmpio, 1973.

Gallet, Luciano. *Estudos de folclore.* Rio de Janeiro: Carlos Wehrs & Companhia, 1934.

Gardel, Luis D. *Escolas de samba.* Rio de Janeiro: Livraria Kosmos, 1967.

Goldwasser, Maria Julia. *O palácio do samba.* Rio de Janeiro: Zahar, 1975.

Goulart, Maurício. *Escravidão africana no Brasil: das origens à extinção do tráfico.* São Paulo: Martins, 1950.

Grandpré, Louis Marie Joseph. *Voyage à la côte occidental d'Afrique fait dans les annés 1786 et 1787.* Paris: Dentu 1801.

Greenberg, Joseph Harold. *Studies in African Linguistic Classification.* Bradford: Compass Publisher, 1955.

_____. *Languages of Africa.* Bloomington: Indiana University, 1963.

_____. "Linguistic Evidence Regarding Bantu Origins." *Journal of African History* 13 (1972): 189-216.

Gurvitch, Georges. *La Vocation Actuelle de la Sociologie*, vol. II. Paris: Presses Universitaires de France, 1963.

_____. *Les Cadres Sociaux de la Connaissance.* Paris: Presses Universitaires de France, 1966.

Guthrie, Malcolm. "Some Developments in the Prehistory of the Bantu Languages." *Jurnal of African History* 3, 2 (1962): 273-283.

_____. "Contributions from Comparative Bantu Studies to the Prehistory of Africa," in *Language and History in Africa* edited by David Dalby. London: Frank Cass and Company Limited, 1970, pp. 20-49.

Halbwachs, Maurice. *Les Cadres Sociaux de la Mémoire*. Paris: Presses Universitaires de France, 1952.

_____. *La Mémoire Collective. Ouvrage posthume publie*. Paris: Presses Universitaires de France, 1950.

_____. *La Mémoire Collective*. Paris: Presses Universitaires de France, 1968.

Herskovits, Melville Jean. "A Preliminary Consideration of the Culture Areas of Africa." *American Anthropologist* XXVI (1924): 50-63.

_____. "The Culture Area of Africa." *Africa III* (1930): 59-70.

_____. "Drums and Drummers in Afro-Brazilian Cult Life." *Musical Quarterly* 30 (1944): 477-492.

_____. "Introduction," in, *Acculturation in the Americas: Proceedings and Selected Papers of the XXIXth International Congress of Americanists*. Chicago: Sol Tax, 1952, pp. 49-63.

_____. *The Myth of the Negro Past*. Boston: Beacon Press, 1958.

_____. "The southernmost outposts of New World Africanisms." *American Anthropologist* 45, 4, 1 (1943): 495-510.

Herskovits, Melville Jean & Waterman, Richard Alan. "Música de culto afro-bahaiano." *Revista de Estudos Musicales* 1 (1949): 65-127.

Hodges, Norman E. W. *Black History*. New York: Monarch Press, 1971.

Hood, Mantle. "The Reliability of Oral Tradition." *Journal of the American Musicological Society* 12, 2-3 (1959): 201-9.

_____. *The Ethnomusicologists*. New York: McGraw Hill, 1971.

Hornbostel, Erich Moritz von. *African Negro Music*. London: Oxford University Press, s.d.

Jacolliot, Louis. *La côte d'ebène: le dernier des négriers.* Paris: Librairie Illustrée, 1876.

Jahn, Janheinz. *Muntu: las culturas neoafricanas.* Buenos Aires: Fondo de Cultura Económica, 1963.

Jones, Arthur Morris "The study of African Musical Rhythm." *Bantu Studies* XI (1935): 295.

_____. "African rhythm." *Africa* XXIV, 1 (1954): 26-47.

_____. *Studies in African Music.* 2 vols. London: Oxford University Press, 1959.

Kaemmer, John E. *Music in Human Life: Anthropological Perspectives on Music.* Austin: University of Texas Press, 1993.

Kagabo Pilipili. "A l'origine des Villes du Zaire: le rôle socio-economique des détribalisés zairois d'avant 1940," in *Likundoli: Enquêtes d'Histoire Zairoise* 1, 1-2 (1972): 25-28.

Kagame, Alexis. "A percepção empírica do tempo e concepção da história no pensamento Bantu." *As Culturas e o Tempo.* São Paulo. Editora da Universidade de São Paulo, 1975, pp. 102-135.

_____. *La philosophie Bantu comparée.* Paris: Présence Africaine, 1976.

Kardinier, Abram. *The Psychological Frontier of Society.* New York: Columbia University Press, 1945.

Kazadi, Pierre Cary. "Game Songs of the Luba-Shankadi Children." Master Thesis, University of California, Los Angeles, 1971.

_____. *The Characteristic Criteria in the Vocal Music of the Luba-Shankadi Children.* Tervuren: Musée Royal de l'Afrique Centrale 75, 1972.

_____. "Trends of the Nineteenth and Twentieth Century Music in the Congo-Zaire," in Gunther, Robert (ed.). *Musikkulturen Asiens, Afrikas und Ozeaniens in 19. Jahrhundert.* Regensburg: Gustav Verlag, 1973, pp. 267-283.

Kazadi wa Mukuna. "The Origin of Zairean Modern Music: A Socio-Economic Aspect," in *African Urban Studies* 6 (Winter 1979-1980): 31-39.

_____. "The Structure of Bantu Praise Songs in Zaire." *Michigan Music Educator,* (April, 1980): 7-8; 18.

_____. "Abordagem interdisciplinaridade em etnomusicologia," in, Morais, Domingues (ed.). *Novas perspectivas em etnomusicologia*. Lisboa: Museu de Etnologia, 1989, pp. 23-7.

_____. "The Process of Assimilation of African Musical Elements in Brazil." *The World of Music 32*, 3 (1990): 104-106.

_____. "Resilience and Transformation in Varieties of African Music in Latin America," in *Festschrift for Gerhard Kubik*. Dietrich Schuler & August Schmiedhofer, Eds. Vienna: Institut für Musikwissenschaft der Universität Wien, 1993, pp. 405-412.

_____. "Resilience and Transformation in Varieties of African Musical Elements in Latin America," in, Schmidhofer, A. & Schuller, D. (eds.). *For Gerhard Kubik: Festschrift on the Occasion of his 60th Birthday*. Wien: Peter Lang, 1994, pp. 405-412.

_____. "Creative Practice in African Music: New Perspectives in the Scrutiny of Africanisms in Diaspora." *Black Music Research Journal 17*, 2 (1997)): 239-250.

_____. "Ethnomusicology and Study of Africanisms in the Music of Latin America," in, *The Heritage of African Music*. Cogdel Djedje Jacqueline (ed.). Los Angeles: University of California Press, 1999, pp. 182-185.

_____. "Ethnomusicology and the African Oral Tradition in Brazil," in *Musica e História no Longo Século XIX* edited by António Herculano Lopes et al. Rio de Janeiro: Casa de Rui Barbosa, 2011, pp. 97-113.

_____. "African Oral Tradition: The Interpretation of Africanisms in Brazil." *Homme, Nature et Patrimonialisation - Le DVD-ROM du Centre d'archives et des documents ethnographiques de la Guyane (CADEG)*. Guyane, 2012.

_____. "The Oral Tradition and the Teaching of African Culture in Brazil: New Challenges and Perspectives," in Homenagem a Professor Mourão, edited by Kabengele Munanga, São Paulo, Brasil (in press).

_____. "Africanisms in the Afro -Brazilian Musical Cultures: A Linguistic Consideration," in *La Música entre África y America*, edited by Coriún Aharonián. Centro Nacional de Documentacion Musical Lauro Ayestarán. Montevideo (Uruguay) - (in press).

Kazadi wa Mukuna & Pinto, Tiago de Oliveira. "The Study of African Musical Contribution to Latin America and the Caribbean: A Methodological Guideline." *Bulletin of the International Committee on Urgent Anthropological and Ethnological Research* 32-3 (1990–1991): 47-8.

Koster, Henry. *Viagens ao nordeste do Brasil*. São Paulo: Companhia Editora Nacional, 1942.

Kubik, Gerhard. "Transmission et transcription des éléments de musique instrumentale africaine." *Bulletin of the International Committee on Urgent Anthropological and Ethnological Research* 11, (1969): 47-61.

———. *Música tradicional e aculturada dos Kungs de Angola*. Lisboa: Junta de Investigação do Ultramar, 1970.

———. "Oral Notation of Some West and Central African Timeline Patters." *Review of Ethnology* 3, 22 (1972): 169-176.

———. *Entensionen Afrikanischer kulturen in Brasilien*. Gottigen: Alano Verlag, 1991.

Lalèyê, Issiaka Prosper. *La conception de la personne dans la pensée traditionnelle Yoruba*. Berne: Herbert Lang, 1970.

Langness, Lewis L. *The Study of Culture*. Third Edition. Npvato, CA: Chandler & Sharp Publishers, 2005.

Laude, Jean. *Les arts de l'Afrique noire*. Paris: Librairie Générale Française, 1966.

Lévi-Strauss, Claude. *Anthropologie structurale*. Paris: Plon, 1958.

Lewis, John Lowell. *Ring of Liberation: Deceptive Discourse in Brazilian Capoeira*. Chicago: University of Chicago Press, 1992.

Lima, Rossini Tavares de. *Folclore de São Paulo*. São Paulo: Ricordi, s.d.

———. *O Folclore do Litoral Norte de São Paulo*. Rio de Janeiro: Ministério da Educação e Cultura, Companhia de Defesa do Folclore Brasileiro, 1968.

———. *Folguedos populares do Brasil*. São Paulo: Ricordi, 1962.

Linton, Ralph. *The Cultural Background of Personality*. London: Routledge & Kegan Paul, 1947.

Lody, Raul Giovanni da Motta. *Ao som de agogô*. Salvador, 1975.

Lopes, Duarte. *Relação do Reino do Congo e das terras circunvizinhas*, Lisbon: Agencia Geral de Ultramar, Divisão de Publicação e Biblioteca, 1951.

Macedo, Sergio D. T. de. *Apontamentos para a história do tráfico negreiro no Brasil*. Rio de Janeiro, 1941.

_____. *Crônica do negro no Brasil*. São Paulo: Record, 1973.

Machado Filho, Aires da Mata. "O negro e o garimpo em Minas Gerais." *Revista do Arquivo Municipal de São Paulo* 5, 63 (1940): 271-98.

Malheiro, Perdigão A. M. *A escravidão africana no Brasil: ensaio históricojurídico-social*. Cadernos de História n° 8. São Paulo: Cultura, 1964.

Malinowski, Bronislaw. "Prologo," in *Contrapunteo Cubano del Tabaco y el Azúcar* by Fernando Ortiz. Barcelona: Editorial Ariel, 1973, pp. 5-15.

Maquet, Jacques N. *Note sur les instruments de musique congolais*. Bruxelles: Académie Royale des Sciences Coloniales, 1958.

_____. *Les civilisations noires*. Paris: Marabout, 1962.

Marconi, Marina de A. "Lundu baiano, desafio coreográfico." *Revista Brasileira de Folclore* 2, 5 (1963): 23-26.

Maultsby, Portia. "Africanism in African-American Music," in Holloway, Joseph E. (ed.). *Africanisms in American Culture*. Bloomington: Indiana University Press, 1990, pp. 185-210.

Meki Nzewi. *Musical Practice and Creativity: An African Traditional Perspective*. Bayreuth: Iwalewa-Haus, Univeristy of Bayreuth, 1971.

Mello, Theodoro Pereira de. *A música no Brasil: desde os tempos coloniais até o primeiro decênio da república*. Bahia, 1908.

Mendes, Júlia de Brito. *Canções populares do Brasil*. Rio de Janeiro: J. Ribeiro dos Santos, 1911.

Mendonça, Renato. *A influência africana no português do Brasil*. Brasília: Civilização Brasileira, 1973.

Merriam, Alan P. "Songs of the Afro-Bahian Cults: an Ethnomusicological Analysis," in, *Summaries of Doctoral Dissertations* (Northwestern University) 19 (1951): 219-223.

_____. *The Anthropology of Music*. Evanston: Northwestern University Press, 1964.

_____. "The Bala Musician," in, d'Azevedo, Warren L. (ed.). *The Traditional Artist in African Societies*. Bloomington: Indiana University Press, 1973, pp. 250-281.

Middleton, John. *Black Africa: Its Peoples and their Cultures Today*. London: Macmillan Company, 1970.

Milheiros, Mário. *Notas de etnografia Angolana*. Luanda; Instituto de Investigação Científica de Angola, 1967.

Miller, Joseph Calder. *Slavery and Slaving in World History: A Bibliography*. Armonk: M. E. Sharpe, 1999.

Morin, Edgar. "Remarques sur la commutation des traits sociaux," in Balandier, George. *Sociologie des mutations*. Paris: Anthropos, 1970, pp. 145-56.

Mourao, Fernando Augusto Albuquerque. "La contribution de l'Afrique Bantoue à la formation de la société brésilienne: une tentative de redéfinition methodologique," in Communication faite à l'Univérsité Nationale du Zaire (Lubumbashi), 1974.

_____. "Reprise de l'Afrique au Brésil," in Communication faite au Colloque sur *Négritude et Amérique Latine* du 7 au 12 Janvier 1974, Dakar (Sénégal).

Murdock, George Peter. *Africa: its Peoples and their Culture History*. New York: McGraw-Hill, 1959.

_____. *De la structure sociale*. Paris: Payot, 1972.

Nery, Frederico José de Santa-Anna. *Folk-lore brésilien*. Paris, 1889.

Nettl, Bruno. *Music in Primitive Cultures*. Cambridge, 1956.

_____. *Theory and Method in Ethnomusicology*. Nova York: The Free Press, 1964.

_____. *The Study of Ethnomusicology: Thirty-one Issues and Concepts*. Urbana: University of Illinois Press, 2005.

_____. *Nettl's Elephant: On the History of Ethnomusicology*. Urbana: University of Illinois Press, c2010.

Newbery, Colin Walter. *The Western Slaves Coast and its Rulers: European Trade and Administration Among the Yoruba and Adja-speaking Peoples of South-western Nigeria, Southern Dahomey and Togo*. Oxford: Clarendon Press, 1961.

Newit, Malyn (ed.). *The Portuguese in West Africa, 1415-1670: A Documentary History.* Cambridge: Cambridge University Press, 2010.

Nketia, Joseph Hanson Kwabena. *Drumming in Akan communities of Ghana.* Edinburgh: T. Nelson, 1963

_____. *The Music of Africa.* New York: Norton, 1974.

_____. *Ethnomusicology and African Music: Modes of Inquiry and Interpretation. Collected Papers, Volume One.* Accra: Afram Publications (Ghana), 2005.

Oliver, Roland. "The Problem of the Bantu Expansion." *Journal of African History* VII (1966): 361-376.

Oliver, Roland & Atmore, Anthony. *Africa since 1800.* Cambridge: Cambridge University Press, 1972.

Oliveira, Ernesto Veiga de. *Instrumentos musicais populares portugueses.* Lisboa: Fundação Calouste Gulbenkian, 1966.

Ortiz, Fernando. *La africania de la música folklórica de Cuba.* Habana: Ediciones Cárdenas y Cia., 1950.

_____. *Los instrumentos de la música Afro-Cubana.* . 5 vols. Habana: Talleres Tipográficos ALFA, 1952.

_____. *Contrapunteo Cubano del Tabaco y el Azúcar.* Barcelona: Editorial Ariel, 1973.

Pereira, João-Batista Borges. *Cor, profissão e mobilidade.* São Paulo: Editora da Universidade de São Paulo, 1967.

Pinto, Tiago de Oliveira. *Capoeira, Samba, Candomblé: Afro-brasilianische Musik in Reconcavo, Bahia.* Berlin: Museums für Volkerkunde, 1991.

Pinto, Virgílio Noya. *O ouro brasileiro e o comércio anglo-português.* Tese de doutoramento. Departamento de História da Universidade de São Paulo, 1972.

Posnansky, Merrick. "Introduction à la fin de la préhistoire en Afrique Subsaharienne," in, *Histoire Générale de l'Afrique* (II), Cap. XXI. Paris, 1976, pp. 575-594.

Querino, Manuel Raymundo. *Costumes africanos no Brasil.* Rio de Janeiro: Civilização Brasileira, 1938.

Radcliffe-Brown, Alfred Reginald. *Structure et fonction dans la société primitive*. Paris: Les Editions de Minuit, 1968.

Ramos, Artur. *As culturas negras no Novo Mundo*. Rio de Janeiro: Civilização Brasileira, 1937.

_____. *The Negro in Brazil*. Washington: Associated Publishers, 1938.

_____. *O negro brasileiro*. São Paulo: Nacional, 1940.

_____. *Introdução à antropologia brasileira*. Rio de Janeiro: Coleção Estudos Brasileiros da Casa dos Estudantes do Brasil, 1943.

_____. *O folclore negro no Brasil*. Rio de Janeiro: Casa dos Estudantes do Brasil, 1954.

Rebelo, Manuel dos Anjos da Silva. *Relações entre Angola e Brasil 1808-1830*. Lisboa: Agencia Geral do Ultramar, 1970.

Rego, Waldeloir. *Capoeira Angola: ensaio sócio-etnográfico*. Salvador: Itapuã, 1968.

Reclus, Elisée. *Nouvelle géographie universelle*. Paris: Hachette, 1876-1894.

Ribeiro, Maria de Lourdes Borges. "Influência de cultura angolense no Vale do Paraíba." *Revista Brasileira de Folclore* 8, 21 (1968): 155-172.

Richelle, Marc. *Aspects psychologiques de l'acculturation : recherche sur les motivations de la stabilisation urbaine au Katanga*. Elisabethville (Congo): Centre d'études des problèmes sociaux indigènes, 1960.

Rinchon, Dieudonné. *Traite et l'esclavage des congolais par les européens; histoire de la déportation de 13.250.000 de noires en Amérique*. Bruxelles: De Meester et Fils, 1929.

_____. *L'organisation commerciale de la traite*. Paris, 1938.

_____. *Pierre-Ignace-Liévin van Alstein, Capitaine Négrier: Gand 1733 - Nantes 1793*. Dakar: Mémoires de l'Institut Français d'Afrique Noire n° 71, 1964.

Rodrigues, Nina R. "As belas artes nos colonos pretos do Brasil." *Kosmos* 1, 8 (1904).

_____. *Os africanos no Brasil*. 2ª edição São Paulo: Editora Nacional, 1935.

Rodrigues, Wilson W. *Folclore coreográfico do Brasil*, São Paulo: Publicitam, s.d.

Rothe, F. F. "The popular music of Brazil." *Brazil* 139 (1940): 12-16.

Ruguendas, Johann Moritz. *Malerische Reise in Brasilien*. Paris: Engelmann & Cie, 1835.

Sachs, Curt. *The History of Musical Instruments*. New York: Norton, 1940.

Saint-Moulin, Louis de. "Les anciens vilages des environs de Kinshasa." *Etudes d'Histoire Africaine 2* (1971): 83-119.

Silva, Antonio de Moraes. *Diccionário da língua portugueza*. Lisboa: Empreza Litterária Fluminense, 1877.

Simonsen, Roberto C. "Recursos econômicos e movimentos das populações." *Revista Brasileira de Estatística* 1, 2 (1940): 199-228.

Stanley, Henry Morton. *The Congo and the Founding of Its Free State: A Story of Work and Exploration*. London: Low, 1885.

Stevenson, Robert. "The Afro-American Musical Legacy to 1800." *Musical Quarterly* 24 (1968): 475-502.

Sutton, J. E. G. "The Aquatic Civilization of Middle Africa." *Journal of African History* XV (1974): 527-546.

Taunay, Alfonso de E. *Subsídios para a história do tráfico africano no Brasil*. São Paulo: Imprensa Oficial do Estado, 1941.

Tempels, Placide. *Bantu philosophy*. Translated by Ver. Colin King. Paris: Présence Africaine, 1959.

Thomas, Luis-Vincent & Luneau, René. *La terre africaine et sés religions: traditions et changements*. Paris: Librairie Larousse, 1975.

Tinhorão, José Ramos. *Música popular: um tema em debate*. Rio de Janeiro: Saga, 1966.

_____. *Música popular*. Petrópolis: Vozes, 1972.

_____. *Pequena história da música popular*. Petrópolis: Vozes, 1974.

UNESCO. *Introdución a la cultura africana em América Latina*. Paris, 1970.

_____. *Union Minière du Haut Katanga 1906-1956*. Bélgica, 1956.

Vansina, Jan. *Le Royaume Kuba*. Kinshasa: Editions Universitaires du Congo, 1964.

_____. *Introduction à l'ethnographie du Congo.* Kinshasa: Editions Universitaires du Congo, 1965.

_____. *Kingdoms of the Savanna.* Madison: The University of Wisconsin Press, 1966.

_____. *The Tio Kingdom of the Middle-Congo (1880-1892).* London: Oxford University Press, 1973.

_____. *Oral Tradition as History.* Madison: The University of Wisconsin Press, 1985.

Vasconcelos, Agripa. *Chico Rei.* Belo Horizonte: Itatiaia, 1966.

Vasconcelos, Ary. *Panorama da música popular brasileira.* São Paulo, 1961.

Verger, Pierre. "Influence du Brésil au Golfe du Benin," in, *Mémoire de l'Institut Français d'Afrique Noire 27,* Dakar, 1953.

_____. *Dieux d'Afrique: culte des Orisha et Vodous à l'ancienne cote des esclaves en Afrique et à Bahia, la baie de tous les Saints au Brésil.* Paris: P. Hartmann, 1954.

_____. *Flux et reflux de la traite des nègres entre le Golfe de Benin et Bahia de todos os Santos du XVII e au XIX siècle.* Paris: Mouton, 1968.

Verhulpen, Edmond. *Baluba et Balubaisés du Katanga.* Anvers: L'Avenir Belge, 1936.

Vianna, Helio. *História do Brasil.* São Paulo: Editora da Universidade de São Paulo, 1975.

Vidal, Ademar. "Congos." *Revista do Brasil, Rio de Janeiro 2,* 8 (1939): 53-62.

Viet, Jean. *Les méthodes structuralistes dans les sciences sociales.* Paris: Mouton, 1965.

Wachsmann, Klauss. "Criteria for Acculturation." *International Musicological Society.* Report of the Eighth Congress. Nova York, 1961, pp. 139-149.

Wagley, Charles. "Regionalism and Cultural Unity in Brazil." *Social Forces 26* (1948): 457-464.

_____. *Race and class in rural Brazil.* Paris: UNESCO, 1952.

Waterman, Richard Alan. "African patterns in Trinidad Negro Music," in *Summaries of Doctoral Dissertations* (Northwestern University) 11 (1943): 57-61.

_____. "African influence on the music of the Americas," in, *Acculturation in the Americas*. Proceedings and Selected Paper of the XXIXth International Congress of Americanists. Chicago: Sol Tax, 1952.

Wetherell, James. *Stray Notes from Bahia*. Liverpool: Web and Hunt, 1900.

Young, Kimball. *Handbook of Social Psychology*. London: Routledge and Kegan Paul, 1948.

Spix, Johann Baptist Von & Martius, Carl Friedrich Phillip Von. *Atlas zur Reise in Brasilien (1817-1820)*. 4 vols. Brazil, s.n., 1938.

NOTES

1. Created in 1947 by Greek businessman Nicolas Jeronimidis and exploited after his death by his brother Alexandre and his son-in-law Nikis Cavvadias, Ngoma was one of the first reputable recording studios in Kinshasa that contributed to the establishment and the definition of style of the modern music of DRC.

2. According to Luís da Câmara Cascudo, *Dicionário do Folclore Brasileiro* (3 a edição, Brasília: Instituto Nacional do Livro, Ministério da Educação e Cultura, 1972, p. 871), *Umbanda* is the current name by which the surviving African religion is known in Brazil.

3. See Jean Duvignaud. *Durkheim: Sa Vie, Son Oeuvre, avec un Exposé de sa Philosophie.* Paris: Presses Universitaires de France, 1965. For an extended discussion on the subject of memory and society, see also Georges Gurvitch. *La Vocation Actuelle de la Sociologie,* vol. II. Paris: Presses Universitaires de France, 1963, and *Les Cadres Sociaux de la Connaissance.* Paris: Presses Universitaires de France, 1966, and Henry Bergson. *Matière et Mémoire,* 2nd ed. Paris: Presses Universitaires de France, 1968.

4. Philip Tagg. "Analyzing Popular Music: Theory, Method, and Practice," in *Reading Pop: Approaches to Textual Analysis in Popular Music,* edited by Richard Middleto. New York: Oxford University Press, 2000, p. 74.

5. Idem., p. 78.

6. John Blacking quoted in Richard Middleton. *Studying Popular Music.* Philadelphia: Open University Press, 2002, p. 146; for further opinions on this matter, see also David Coplan quoted in this same source on page 147.

7. Many are the dates proposed by the scholars regarding the arrival of Diogo Cão and his expedition at the mouth of the Congo River. Among others, Stanley put this event in a period between 1484–85, while most writers confirm that they arrived in 1482, David Birmingham (1965) proposes 1483; Perdigão A. M. Malheiro. *A escravidão africana no Brasil: ensaio histórico-jurídico-social.* Cadernos de Historia no. 8. São Paulo: Cultura, 1964, pp. 13-14, 16.

8. Louis Jacolliot. *La cote d'ébène: le dernier des négriers.* Paris: Librairie Illustrée, 1876, p. 115.

9. Georges Balandier. *La vie quotidienne au royaume de Kongo du XVIe au XVIIIe*

siècle. Paris: Hanchette, 1965, p. 16.

10. Elisée Reclus. *Nouvelle Géographie Universelle.* Paris: Hachette, 1876–1894, p. 199.

11. Ibid., pp. 199–200.

12. Dieudonné Rinchon. *Pierre-Ignace-Liévin van Alstein, Capitaine Negrier. Gand 1733—Nantes 1793.* Dakar: Mémoires de l'Institut Français d'Afrique Noire no. 71, 1964, p. 36.

13. Georges Balandier, op. cit., p. 16.

14. Charles Ralph Boxer. *Salvador de Sá e a luta pelo Brasil e Angola 1602–1686.* São Paulo: Editora da Universidade de São Paulo, 1973, p. 237.

15. Robert and Marianne Cornevin. *Histoire de l'Afrique des origines à la deuxième guerre mondiale.* Paris: Payot, 1964, p. 193.

16. Edmond Verhulpen. *Baluba et Balubaisés du Katanga.* Anvers: L'Avenir Belge, 1936; Le Révérend Père Colle. *Les Baluba (Congo Belge): Sociologie Descriptive.* Bruxelles: A. De Wit: Institut International de Bibliographie, 1936.

17. See also Balandier, op. cit., p. 18; compare with Kazadi wa Mukuna. "The Structure of Bantu Praise Songs in Zaire." *Michigan Music Educator* (April 1980:7–8); lecture given at the Centro de Estudos Afro-Orientais da Universidade Federal da Bahia, in August, 1975.

18. Paiva Manso mentioned in Balandier, op. cit., pp. 17–18.

19. Jan Vansina. *Kingdoms of the Savanna.* Madison: University of Wisconsin Press, 1966, p. 38.

20. Balandier, op. cit., p. 16.

21. Cuvelier, cited in Balandier, op. cit., p. 17.

22. Dapper, cited by Balandier, op. cit., p. 17.

23. Compare with Vansina, op. cit. Chapter II.

24. Banana, taro, and yam.

25. Greenberg, cited in George Peter Murdock. *Africa: Its Peoples and Their Culture History.* New York: McGraw-Hill, 1959, p. 271.

26. Joseph Harold Greenberg. *The Languages of Africa.* Bloomington: Indiana University Press, 1963, p. 7.

27. Mudock, op. cit., pp. 271–272.

28. Murdock, op. cit., p. 273.

29. Ibid., p. 274.

30. Raymond A. Dart. *Bantu-Speaking Societies of South Africa: An Ethnographical Survey*, 6th edition. London: Routledge & Kegan Paul, 1959, pp. 1–28.

31. Dart, op. cit., pp. 6–7.

32. Ibid., p. 7.

33. Christopher Ehret. "Bantu Origins and History: Critique and Interpretation." *Transafrican Journal of History* 2 (1972), p. 14.

34. Merrick Posnansky. "*Introduction à la fin de la préhistoire en Afrique subsaharienne*," in *Histoire Générale de l'Afrique*. Paris: UNESCO: Nouvelles Editions Africaines, 1976, p. 585.

35. Jacques Nenquin. "Notes on Some Early Pottery Cultures in Northern Katanga." Journal of African History, IV, 1963; David Birmingham. "The Date and Significance of the Imbangala Invasion of Angola." *Journal of African History* 6, 2 (1965); Malcolm Guthrie. "Some Developments in the Prehistory of Bantu Languages." *Journal of African History* 3, 2 (1962), p. 2.

36. David Birmingham. "The Date and Signification of the Imbangala Invasion of Angola." *Journal of African History* 6, 2 (1985), p. 143.

37. Vansina, op. cit., p. 25.

38. Compare with Vansina, op. cit., p. 30.

39. Balandier, op. cit., p. 14.

40. Louis de Saint Moulin. "Les anciens villages des environs of Kinshasa." *Etudes d'Histoire Africaine* 2 (1971), p. 95.

41. Verhulpen paraphrasing in Pierre C. Kazadi. *The Characteristic Criteria in the Vocal Music of the Luba-Shankadi Children*. Tervuren: Musée Royal de l'Afrique Centrale, 1972, pp. 5–6; cf., also, David Birmingham. "The Date and Significance of the Imbangala Invasion of Angola." *Journal of African History*, VI (1965), p. 151.

42. Birmingham, op. cit., p. 150.

43. Kazadi, op. cit., p. 6.

44. Verhulpen, cited in Pierre C. Kazadi. "Game Songs of the Luba-Shankadi

Children." Master Thesis. University of California, Los Angeles, 1971, p. 7.

45. Verhulpen, cited in Kazadi 1971, p. 7.

46. Birmingham, op. cit., pp. 24–25.

47. David A. Birmingham. *A conquista portuguesa de Angola*. Porto: A Regra do Jogo, 1965, p. 25.

48. Vansina, op. cit., p. 67.

49. Giovanni A. Cavazzi. *Istorica descrizione de' tre regni Congo, Matamba, et Angola*. Bologna: Giovani Monti, 1687, pp. 182–186.

50. Vansina, op. cit., p. 67.

51. R. Avelot and H. C. Desker in Vansina 1966, p. 67.

52. William Fagg. *Sculptures Africaines: les univers artistique des tribus d'Afrique Noire*. Paris: F. Harzan, c. 1965, pp. 17–18.

53. Fagg, op. cit., pp. 16-17.

54. For an in-depth analysis of the subject, see Kazadi wa Mukuna, "The Structure of Bantu Praise Songs in Zaire" in *Michigan Music Educator*, April 1980:7–8. This was written on the conference given in the Centro de Estudos Afro-Orientais from Universidade Federal da Bahia, in August 1975.

55. Rui de Pina cited in Robert Stevenson. "The Afro-American musical legacy to 1800." *Musical Quarterly* 24, 1968, p. 478.

56. Vansina, op. cit., p. 48.

57. Perdigão A. M. Malheiro. *A escravidão africana no Brasil: ensaio histórico-jurídico-social*. Cadernos de Historia no. 8, São Paulo: Cultura, 1964, p. 15.

58. Malheiro, op. cit., p. 17.

59. Ibid., p. 12.

60. Pierre Verger. *Flux et reflux de la traite des negres entre le Golfe de Benin et Bahia de todos os Santos du XVIIe e au XIXe siècle*. Paris: Mouton, 1968, p. 9.

61. Dieudonné Rinchon. *Pierre-Ignace-Liévin van Alstein, Capitaine Negrier: Gand 1733-Nantes 1793*. Dakar: Mémoires de l'Institut Français d'Afrique Noire no. 71, 1964, p. 37.

62. Paiva Meek cited in Balandier, op. cit., pp. 72–73.

63. Balandier, op. cit, p. 72.

64. See also Maurice Halbwachs. *La memoire collective.* Paris: Presses Universitaires de France, 1968, p. vii.

65. Ibid., p. 77.

66. Charles Ralph Boxer. *Salvador de Sa e a luta pelo Brasil e Angola 1602-1686.* São Paulo: Editora de Universidade de São Paulo, 1973, p. 242.

67. Boxer, op. cit., p. 243.

68. David Birmingham. *A conquista portuguesa de Angola.* Porto: A Regra do Jogo, 1965, p. 12.

69. Boxer, op. cit., p. 243.

70. Maurice Halbwachs. *Les cadres sociaux de la mémoire.* Paris: Presses Universitaires de France, 1952, p. 33.

71. Halbwachs, 1950, p. xi.

72. Halbwachs, 1968, p. 292.

73. Cf. Verger, 1968, p. 11.

74. Roberto Cochrane Simonsen. "Recursos económicos e movimentos das populações." *Revista Brasileira de Estatística* 1, 2 (1940), p. 205.

75. Pierre Verger. *Flux et reflux de la traite des nègres entre le golfe de Benin et Bahia de todos os santos, du XVIIe aux XIX siècle.* Paris: Mouton, 1968, p. 11.

76. Compare with Melville J. Herskovits. "The Southernmost Outposts of New World Africanisms." *American Anthropologist* 45, 4, 1 (1943), p. 497.

77. Verger, op. cit., p. 13.

78. Roger Bastide. *Les Amériques Noires.* Paris: Payot, 1967, pp. 14-15.

79. Among others, Louis D. Gardel. *Escolas de samba.* Rio de Janeiro: Livraria Kosmos, 1967; Sérgio Cabral. *As escolas de samba: o que, quem, como, quando e por que.* Rio de Janeiro: Fontana, 1974; Rossini Tavares de Lima. *Folclore de São Paulo.* São Paulo: Ricordi, s.d.; João Baptista Borges de Pereira. *Cor, profissão e mobilidade; o negro e o rádio de São Paulo.* São Paulo: Editora da Universidade de São Paulo, 1967.

80. Edison Carneiro. *Samba de umbigada.* Rio de Janeiro: Ministério da Educação e Cultura, 1961, p. 11.

81. Cited in Edison Carneiro, op. cit., p. 10.

82. Cited in Edison Carneiro, op. cit., p. 11.

83. Ibid., p. 55.

84. Gardel, op. cit., p. 6.

85. Ibid., p. 122.

86. Cardel, op. cit., p. 126.

87. José Ramos Tinhorão. *Música popular: um tema em debate.* Rio de Janeiro: Saga, 1966, p. 9.

88. Quoted in Carneiro, op. cit., p. 17.

89. Gerard Béhague. "The Lundu and the Modinha of Brazil in the 19th Century." *Symposium of the College Music Society*, 7 (Fall 1967): 103-6.

90. Interviewed July 19, 1975 in Rio de Janeiro.

91. Gardel, op. cit., p. 122.

92. Pereira, op. cit., pp. 215-216.

93. Ibid., pp. 216-217.

94. Ibid., p. 224.

95. Edison Carneiro. *Carta do Samba.* Rio de Janeiro: Ministério da Educação e Cultura, 1962, p. 3.

96. Rafael J. de Menezes. "Las músicas tradicionales del Brasil." *Revista Musical Chilena* 28, 125 (1974), p. 30.

97. Luís de Câmara Cascudo. *Dicionário de folclore brasileiro* 2nd ed. Rio de Janeiro: Instituto Nacional do Livro, 1962, p. 200.

98. Waldeloir Rego. *Capoeira Angola: ensaio sócio-etnográfico.* Salvador: Itapuã, 1968, p. 87.

99. Fernão Cardim. *Tratado da terra e da gente do Brasil.* São Paulo: Companhia Editora Nacional, 1939, p. 301.

100. António de Moraes Silva. *Dicionário da língua portuguesa.* Lisboa: Empresa Literária Fluminense, 1877, p. 341.

101. Henry Koster. *Viagens ao nordeste do Brasil.* São Paulo: Companhia Editora

NOTES

Nacional, 1942, p. 333.

102. Ibid., pp. 316–317.

103. Op. cit., p. 72.

104. *Instrumentos musicais populares portugueses.* Lisboa: Calouste Gulbenkin, 1966, p. 222.

105. See Joseph Harold Greenberg. *Studies in African Linguistic Classification.* New Haven, 1955; *The Languages of Africa.* Bloomington: Indiana University Press, 1963.

106. J. H. Kwabena Nketia. *The Music of Africa.* New York: Norton, 1974, p. 7.

107. Francis Bebey. *Musique de l'Afrique.* Paris: Horizons de France, 1969, p. 57.

108. A. M. Jones, cited in Pierre Cary *Kazadi. The Characteristic Criteria in the Vocal Music of the Luba-Shankadi Children.* Tervuren: Musée Royal de l'Afrique Centrale, 1972, p. 59.

109. Cf. Ibid.

110. Pierre Cary Kazadi. "Game Songs of the Luba-Shankadi Children." Masters thesis, University of California, Los Angeles, 1971.

111. Pierre Cary Kazadi. "Trends of nineteenth and twentieth century music in the Congo-Zaire," in *Musikkulturen Asiens, Afrikas und Ozeaniens im 19. Jahrhundert*, edited by Robert Gunther. Regensburg: Gustav Verlad, 1973, pp. 267–83.

112. Cited Kazadi, 1971, p. 60.

113. See comparison in Idem.

114. Nketia, op. cit., p. 152.

115. Nketia, op. cit., p. 141.

116. Ibid., p. 183.

117. See Kazadi, 1973, p. 273.

118. Jones, op. cit., p 59.

119. Nketia, op. cit., p. 7.

120. Idem.

121. Gerhard Kubik. *Música tradicional e aculturada dos Kung de Angola.* Lisboa:

Junta de Investigação do Ultramar, 1970, p. 45.

122. Nketia, op. cit., p. 81.

123. Nketia, op. cit., p. 72.

124. Bebey, op. cit., p. 126.

125. Henrique Augusto Dias de Carvalho. *Ethnographia e história tradicional dos povos da Lunda.* Lisboa: Imprensa Nacional 1890, p. 369.

126. See also Bruno Nettl. *Music in Primitive Culture.* Cambridge: Harvard University Press, 1959.

127. Kubik, op. cit., p. 30.

128. Ibid., pp. 19–20.

129. Kubik, op. cit., p. 24.

130. Ibid., p. 27.

131. Fernando Ortiz. *Los instrumentos de la música Afro-Cubana.* 5 vols. Habana: Talleres Tipográficos ALFA, 1952, pp. 17–22.

132. Sachs, cited in Oliveira, op. cit., p. 218.

133. Oliveira, op. cit., p. 218.

134. Ibid., p. 216.

135. Oliveira, op. cit., p. 216; see also Curt Sachs. *The History of Musical Instruments.* New York: Norton, 1940, p. 39; compare with Ortiz (1952), talking in respect of these direct fricatives in Haiti, to accompany the dances in the feasts of fertility.

136. Ortiz, paraphrased in Oliveira, op. cit., p. 215.

137. Hornbostel paraphrased in Oliveira, op. cit., p. 218.

138. Oliveira, op. cit., p. 219.

139. Oliveira, op. cit., p. 219.

140. Edgar Morin. "Remarques sur la communication des traits sociaux," in George Balandier, *Sociologie des mutations.* Paris: Anthropos, 1970, p. 153.

141. Balandier, 1970, p. 17.

142. Roger Bastide. "Le principe de coupure et le comportement afro-brésilien,"

Anais do XXXI Congresso Internacional de Americanistas I, 1954, p. 494.

143. Roger Bastide. *Le prochain et le lointain*. Paris: Cujas, 1970, p. 161.

144. Balandier, op. cit., p. 16.

145. Morin, op. cit., p. 152.

146. Idem.

147. Ibid, p. 153.

148. Levi-Strauss paraphrased in Louis Martin. "Présentation," in Alfred Reginald Radcliffe-Brown, *Structure et fonction dans la société primitive*. Paris: Les Editions de Minuit, 1968, p. 18.

149. Roger Bastide. "La causalité externe et la causalité dans l'explication sociologique," *Cahiers Internationaux de Sociologie*, 21 (1956), p. 77.

150. Balandier, op. cit., pp. 31–4; Mantle Hood, *The Ethnomusicologists*. New York: McGraw Hill, 1971, pp. 300–9.

151. Alan P. Merriam. *The Anthropology of Music*. Evanston: Northwestern University Press, 1964, p. 7.

152. Balandier, op. cit., p. 37.

153. Abram Kardiner. *The Psychological Frontier of Society*. New York: Columbia University Press, 1945, p. vii.

154. Bastide, op. cit., p. 145.

155. George Balandier. *Anthropo-Logiques*. Paris: Presses Universitaires de Fance, 1974, pp. 189–190.

156. See Kazadi wa Mukuna. "The Origin of Zairean Modern Music: A Socio-Economic Aspect," in, *African Urban Studies* 6 (Winter 1979–1980): 31–39.

157. Rose Brandel. *The Music of Central Africa*. The Hague: Martinus Nijhoff, 1961, p. 20.

158. This philosophical concept is discussed at large in Placide Tempels. *Bantu Philosophy*. Translated by Reverend Colin King. Paris: Présence Africaine, 1959; Alexis Kagame. *La philosophie Bantu comparée*. Paris: Présence Africaine, 1976; see also George Balandier. *La vie quotidienne au royaume de Kongo du XVIe au XVIIIe siècle*. Paris: Hachette, 1965, chapter IV, and compare with Kazadi wa Mukuna. "The Structure of Bantu Praise Songs in Zaire." *Michigan Music Educator* (April

1980), pp. 7–8.

159. Roger Bastide. *Les Amériques Noires.* Paris: Payot, 1967, pp. 113–14.

160. Brandel, op. cit., p. 20.

161. Three musical examples taken from P. C. Kazadi (1972); for more examples, see this reference.

162. Bastide paraphrased in Luis-Vincent Thomas et René Luneau. *La terre africaine et ses religions: traditions et changements.* Paris: Librairie Larousse, 1975, p. 34; see also Balandier, 1965, pp. 195–96.

163. See Brandel, op. cit., p. 26.

164. Song lyrics taken from Kazadi, 1972, pp. 69–70.

165. Amadou Hampaté Bâ, "The Living Tradition," in *General History of Africa: Methodology and African Prehistory* edited by Joseph Ki-Zerbo. Los Angeles: University of California Press, 1981, p. 168.

166. Thomas and Luneau, op. cit., p. 37.

167. Lalèyê quoted in Thomas and Luneau, 1975, p. 37.

168. See also Alexis Kagame. "A percepção empírica do tempo e a concepção da história no pensamento Bantu" *As Culturas e o Tempo.* São Paulo: Editora da Universidade de São Paulo, 1975, pp. 109–12.

169. Kubik, op. cit., p. 30.

170. Ortiz, cited in Oliveira, op. cit., 217.

171. Idem.

172. Ibid.

173. Balandier, 1974, p. 190.

174. This element and all about the modern music of Zaire are taken out of Kazadi wa Mukuna. "The Origin of Zairean Modern Music: A Socio-Economic Aspect," *African Urban Studies: Readings in African Urban Music* 6 (Winter 1979–80):31–39.

175. Robert Cornevin. *Le Zaire, ex-Congo-Kinshasa.* Paris: Presses Universitaires de France, 1972, p. 32.

176. *Union Minière du Haut Katanga 1906–1956.* Bruxelles: Belgica, 1956, p. 197.

177. S. Alexandre-Pyre. "L'origine de la population du centre urbain de Lubumbashi," *Publications de l'Université Officielle du Congo à Lubumbashi* 19 (1969), p. 150.

178. cf. Kazadi wa Mukuna "On the Origin of Zaire (Congolese) Modern Music," unpublished article.

179. Alexandre-Pyre, op. cit., p. 143.

180. Balandier, 1970, p. 30.

181. See Radcliffe-Brown, 1968.

182. Henry Pratt Fairchild. *Diccionario de Sociologia.* Mexico: Fondo de Cultura Economica, 1949, p. 66.

183. Herskovits, 1958, p. xxiii.

184. Bastide, 1967, p. 95.

185. Tempels, 1959.

186. Oliveira, E. V. "Introdução." *Escultura Africana no Museu de Ethnologia do Ultramar*, 1968.

187. Mons J. Cuvelier cited in Balandier, 1965, pp. 26–27.

188. Balandier, 1965, p. 27.

189. Kazadi wa Mukuna. "The Structure of Bantu Praise Songs in Zaire." *Michigan Music Educator* (April 1980), pp. 7–8.

190. Pierre Cary Kazadi, op. cit., 1971.

191. Oliveira, op. cit., "Introduction."

192. Herskovits cited in Bastide 1967, p. 8.

193. See Halbwachs, *Mémoire collective*; also, *Les cadres sociaux de la mémoire*.

194. Bastide, 1960, pp. 233–234.

195. Gerhard Kubik, 1970.

196. Frazier cited in Norman E. W. Hodges. *Black History.* New York: Monarch Press, 1971, pp. 60–61.

INDEX

A

acculturation   38, 99-100, 127, 142, 148, 155
adufe   64, 92
Afonso (ruler of Kongo)   19, 21
African Americans   37-8, 135
African-Brazilian religions   65
African coast   1, 8, 84, 120
African cultural elements   37-8, 135
African cultural groups   39, 118
African musical traits   39
African societies   4, 55, 59, 84, 87, 90-1, 101, 111, 124, 130-1, 133, 153
Africanisms   37, 127, 132, 136, 150, 152
agogô   39-40, 56, 63, 69-71, 87, 115, 122, 152
agricultural activities   7, 25, 27-9
Ambundu   14-15 *see also* Mbundu
ancestors   8, 17, 86, 103, 107, 112, 128-30
Angola   1, 4, 14-16, 20, 27-9, 31, 39-41, 58, 65, 80, 88, 114-15, 133-4, 143-5, 162-3
Angola regions   71
Arabs   22, 90
area
  coastal   23, 87-8
  mining   29, 41, 84
Associação Brasileira das Escolas de Samba (ABES)   51
Association Internationale des Sociologues de Langue Française   97-8
Association Internationale des Sociologues de Langue Française (AISLF)   97-8
Aunt Ciata   51
autonomous groups   12, 14

B

Bahia   1, 19, 28, 31, 39, 45-7, 58, 60, 90, 134-5, 147, 152, 154, 157-8, 162-3
Bakongo   11, 14, 16, 22, 56, 69, 71, 85-8, 91-2, 116, 129

171

societies   31
Bakuba   15-16, 91, 116, 130
Balandier, George   5, 11-12, 22, 88, 98, 100-1, 118, 142, 153, 160-3, 166-9
Baluba   12-13, 157, 160
bampamba   102-3, 113-14
Bantu
  ancestors   7, 10, 30
  of Angola   133
  concept of dual identity   104, 123
  identity   128
  languages   9-10
  musical elements in Brazil   122
  nucleus of existence   131-2
  origin   31, 39, 46, 55, 60, 132
  philosophy   11, 17, 37, 103-4, 106, 111-12, 123, 128, 131, 156, 167
  regions   20, 56, 83, 90, 121, 139
  rhythmic pattern   79
  societies   10, 17, 65, 91, 136
  western   93
Bantu, Africa   122
baqueta   62
basket rattle   76, 85, 87-8, 102, 113, 122, 133-4
Bastide, Roger   37-8, 97-8, 100, 103, 106, 127, 132, 142, 163, 166-9
Bateke   4, 11, 22
batuque   41-2, 45-6, 48
Batwa   7, 66, 88
Bayeke   109-10
beliefs   11, 23, 111, 117, 127
bell, double   56, 85-6, 115, 122, 131
Benin   87, 157, 162-3
berimbau   59-63, 88, 90, 114, 122-3, 133-4
bikashi   75-6
Birmingham, David   10, 12-14, 24, 143, 159, 161-3
Boletín Latino Americano   141
Bolia   13
bombo   52, 54
borders   1, 7, 12-13, 71, 84, 120
bow   6, 59, 62-3, 86, 89, 133 *see also under berimbau*
Brasileiros   141-2, 155

Brazil   18-20, 22-4, 27-9, 31-2, 37-8, 41, 43-4, 48-9, 55-6, 58-61, 86-7, 89-90, 114-15, 121-2, 133-6
  the popular music of   156
  rural   158
Brazilian(s)   37-9, 46, 55, 60, 65, 68, 79, 117, 121, 132
  cuíca   117 *see also cuíca*
  culture   139
  folklore   52
  friction drum   63, 93
  historians   41
  life   18, 23, 32
  national character   136
  of African descent   37
  puita   117
  sambas   55 *see also samba*
  scholars   46
  slavery   23, 27, 136
  society   122, 137
  white   60
bumba-meu-boi   134

C

cabula   68-9, 72
camps   14, 72, 119-20, 135
  labor   119, 121, 135
  worker   119, 121, 135
capoeira   50, 58-63, 133-7, 154
  Angola   39, 59, 155, 164
captives (enslaved Africans)   24-5
Carneiro, Edison   41, 43, 46, 51, 133, 163-4
carriers (of culture)   117, 121-4, 128, 132, 139
caxixi   59, 63, 87, 89, 122, 133
Ceará (Brazil)   134-5
Central Africa   14, 66, 72, 83, 88, 143, 167
Central Sudan   9-10
ceremonies   42, 72, 78, 86-7, 91, 101-2, 108, 111, 113-14, 116, 128
Chad   66-7

173

children   11, 14, 30, 49, 78, 106, 108, 114-15, 129, 132, 149, 162
choir   82, 92, 104
Chokwe   80, 84, 86, 89, 115
chorus   76-7, 104
clans   4, 13, 23, 111, 113-14, 128-9
clapper   85-6, 102, 131
class, ruling   93, 136
coastal regions   8, 15-16, 22-4, 26, 66, 68, 88
coconut shell   61-2
coffee, cultivation of   30, 46
coffee culture   49, 134
collective memories   18, 23-4, 26-7, 99, 124-5, 132
communities   59-60, 111, 115, 129-30
   isolated   29-30
Confederação Brasileira das Escolas de Samba   51
conformity   100-1, 118
   enslaved African's   118
Congo   3-4, 15-16, 18-20, 27-8, 31, 38-40, 68, 71-2, 75, 80-1, 86-7, 109-10, 119-21, 129-30, 155-7
   lower   15-16, 65, 71, 88, 115
   modern music of   81, 121
   societies of   11, 31, 72
   southern   19, 80
Congo-Angola
   border   14, 65, 80, 115
   origin   90
   region of cultural interaction   38
Congo-Angola region   41, 47-8, 56, 65, 67, 71, 79, 86-7, 92-3, 117
Congo Basin   4, 11-12, 15-16, 21-3, 42, 87, 101, 122, 128, 139
Congo Railway   119, 135
Congo rhythmic pattern   40
Congo River   1, 4, 11-12, 16, 18, 22, 115, 159
Congo-Zaire   149, 165
continuity   23, 27, 37, 95, 97, 99-100, 113, 118-19, 123-4, 127-8, 131-2, 136-7, 140, 142
core   24, 98-9, 125, 127-8
   conceptual   124-5
   psychic   99
cosmos   111-12, 118, 122-5, 131

INDEX

Cuba 90, 116-17, 154
cuíca 60, 63-4, 90-3, 117, 122
cultural
  common denominators 10, 16, 18, 25, 56, 86, 139
  contacts 65, 127-8
  elements 15, 23, 27, 83, 97, 99, 117-19, 121-3, 125, 131, 139
  groups 17, 31, 38-9, 66, 92, 100-1, 113-14, 132
  inventory 23, 25, 121, 133
  practices 11, 71, 98, 103, 118, 133, 135
  psychology 100
  traits 18, 23, 39, 98, 127-8 *see also* cultural elements
currency 62-3

D

Dakar 153, 155, 157, 160, 162
death 11, 14, 16-17, 91, 104, 106, 112, 115, 159
depersonalization, process of 122, 125, 128
Dibwe diambula kabanda 77-8
diffusion 7, 55, 64, 80, 83, 88, 90, 92, 118
díkàsà 87, 102-3, 113
dispersion 9-10
distribution 7, 84-5, 87-8, 120
  geographical 16, 66-7
Donga 46, 51
drums 42, 54, 61, 63, 72, 76-7, 85-6, 91, 116, 123, 130, 148

E

emancipation 27, 30
empires 3-4, 8, 12-13
enslaved Africans 1, 4, 8, 18-31, 37, 47, 56, 93, 121, 132-5, 147, 152, 159, 162
  emancipated 46, 49
  imported 19
  released 30
  sick 25
enslavement 4, 118, 122-3 *see also* Brazilian slavery and transatlantic slaving

175

escolas   51, 143, 163
Ethnomusicology   150, 153
Europe   55, 60, 90-1
Europeans   11-12, 39, 137
evil   21, 102
existence   17-18, 26, 29, 80, 92, 98-101, 111-12, 119-20, 122-3, 128, 131-2, 134, 139
  nucleus of   131
expression   47, 51, 98, 103, 111, 113, 137
  artistic   10, 12-13, 18, 38, 56, 119
  musical   16, 38, 79-80, 102, 122, 133, 135

F

fandango   52-3
Fluminense region (Brazil)   30, 49
France   60, 91, 142-3, 145-8, 159, 163, 165, 168
friction drum   60, 64, 87, 92, 115-17, 122, 136
functional societies   99, 101, 131

G

Générale Carrière des Mines   119
gold (mining)   27-8
gourd   59, 61, 63, 75, 89

H

Halbwachs, Maurice   18, 23, 25-6, 132, 148, 163, 169
harmony   67, 111-12, 130
Herskovits, Melville   37, 66, 127, 131-2, 142, 148, 163, 169
hierarchical structure   128-30
high tones   56, 70, 86
historians   4, 11
history   25, 27, 111, 139

INDEX

I

Imbangala   13-15, 20-1, 161
improvisation   75-6
initiation   39, 42, 72, 104, 116
  ceremonies   87, 116
Institut Français   155, 160, 162
instrument
  idiophone   84
  mbulumbumba   114
  monotone   67
  sacred   91
instrumental resources   55, 84, 86
instrumentation   41, 102
intermediaries   128-9
invocation   56, 72, 86, 102-3, 113, 116

K

kachacha   80
Kagame, Alexis   123, 149, 167-8
Kasai Region   16, 75, 80, 84-8, 92, 114-15, 121
Kasai River   13-14, 16
Katanga   10, 12, 84, 155, 157, 160-1
Kazadi wa Mukuna   105, 149, 160-2, 165, 167-9
keys (musical)   84-5
kinfwiti   116-17
Kingdom of Kongo   1, 3-5, 11-12, 14-15, 18-21, 26, 65, 75, 79, 92, 129
kings   14, 19, 21, 60, 129-30
Kinguri   14
Kinshasa   11, 42, 119, 156-7, 159, 161
Kongo
  court   93, 129
  second Kingdom of   6, 18
Kongolo   13
Kuba (*see also* Bakuba)   4, 6, 11-12, 15-16, 75, 87, 91-2, 102-3, 115-16, 128, 130
Kubik, Gerhard   80, 84, 88-90, 114, 133, 151, 166, 168
Kwango-Kwilu Basin   16

L

labor, division of   129-30
language families   7, 9, 26, 28, 65, 117, 124, 144, 148, 161
Languages of Africa   147, 160, 165
Latin America   144, 150
Lau clan   129
leaders   4, 14, 19, 128-9
  societal   128
likembe   84
lineages   103, 130
lion   91, 116, 128
Lisbon   18, 20, 47, 90, 143-4, 146, 150-2, 154-6, 164-6
local-regional styles   51, 68, 134
London   144-5, 148-9, 151, 153, 156-8, 161
Luba (*see also* Baluba)   4, 10-16, 42-3, 56, 75-6, 87, 102-4, 107, 113-14, 128, 130, 133
Luba Empire, first   12-13
Lubumbashi   16, 87, 141, 153, 169
Luluwa   80-1, 114
Lunda   4, 6, 14, 75, 80, 84, 86, 115, 144, 166
lundu   44, 46-9, 52-3, 79, 134, 141-3, 164
lunkomba   133-4

M

manikongo (Kongo ruler)   2, 5, 18
maracatu   134
marimba   59, 82, 87
marriage   11, 23, 30, 42, 108, 132
Masanga   109, 121
masks   111
Mato Grosso   29, 147
Mayombe   4, 20, 75
mbenga   42-3
mbira   84-5
Mbundu   19-21, 26, 115
memory   24-5, 50, 124, 131-2, 136, 139, 159

INDEX

collective frames of 25-6
individual 23-4, 26, 119, 131
merchants 8, 19, 21, 25, 75, 92
Mestre Noronha 61-3
migration 7-9, 13, 15-16, 23, 27, 31, 46
  internal 27, 134-5
  massive 27-8
Minas Gerais 28-31, 60, 136, 152
missionaries 18-19
Mobutu Sese Seko 110
modinha 46-9, 52, 79, 134, 142-3, 164
Morin, Edgar 97-8, 153, 166-7
motifs 54, 56, 69-70, 72-4, 81, 104, 122
mountains 17, 103, 106-7
Mpamba wa Bitole 79
muntu 11, 17, 33, 106-7, 109, 124, 128-9, 131, 149
music
  modern 42, 119, 135, 168-9
  vocal 105, 149, 161
musical
  bow 59-61, 88, 90, 115, 122
  forms 47, 134-5
  instruments 60-1, 65-8, 72, 84, 101, 113-14, 117, 122, 124, 130-1, 156
  structure 99, 104
  styles 66, 68, 134
  traces 84, 101, 113
  traits 65, 67, 101, 118
musical cultures 39, 65, 67-8, 73, 75, 80, 82, 84, 88, 113-14
  traditional 67-8
  various 74, 87
mutation 95, 97-100, 115, 117, 119, 124-5, 127, 139, 142, 153, 166
  conceptual 97, 122, 139
Mutumbi 56, 76-7
Mwaku waku Nani 43
Mwana bene 108
myth 10, 13, 23, 37, 112, 127, 146, 148

N

nations 3, 49, 101, 134, 136-7
network 119, 122, 125, 128-9
Nigeria 40, 67, 74
Nketia, J. H. Kwabena 74, 84-5, 154, 165-6
Nsaku 129
Nunes, Clara 57-8

O

oral tradition 4, 43, 71, 74, 84, 111, 148, 150, 157
orchestration 53-4, 85
organization 39, 49, 73, 75-6, 82, 101, 114, 120, 137
  melodic 52

P

pantomime 42, 49
Paraíba (Brazil) 30-1, 44-7, 49, 134, 155
percussion instruments 42, 50, 59, 85
Pernambuco 31, 44, 46
persistence 95, 97, 99, 116-18, 123-4, 127-8, 135, 139
  of Bantu musical elements 128, 132
plantations, sugarcane 19-20, 27
police 50-1, 136
popular music 39, 46, 55-6, 60, 65, 68, 109, 122, 159
ports 4, 28, 30, 119
Portugal 1, 18-20, 47-8, 60, 64, 80, 90-2, 136
Portuguese
  influence 67, 88
  in West Africa 154
Portuguese Empire 1, 6, 18
power 2, 8, 103, 113, 129
process, detribalization 120, 125
pulses 80-3, 88, 113-14, 121, 133-4

Q

INDEX

quavers 54, 70, 80

R

rattles 59, 67, 75, 77, 87-8
Recife (Brazil) 143
relationships 18, 99, 102, 112, 119, 122, 124-5, 129
  hierarchical 130-1
religious practices 11, 116-17
repertoire 72, 75, 101, 104, 107-9, 121, 133
resonator 61-3, 89
revolution 97-8, 110
rhythmic 48, 54-5, 65, 75
  cycles 53, 71-2
  organization 39, 54, 68, 72, 74
  patterns 40, 59, 68, 72, 79-80, 101-2, 113, 117, 121-2, 130-1, 134
Rio de Janeiro 27-31, 45-7, 49, 51, 60, 133-4, 137, 141-4, 147, 150-2, 155-7, 163-4
rites 104, 108, 111-12, 122
  puberty 101-3
riti (Wolof of Senegal) 67
ritual 30, 113-15, 122, 131, 147
rod 62-4, 90-1, 115-16, 123
roda 44-6, 61
Rodrigues, Nina 38, 156
rubembe 86
rupture 97-8, 120, 124-5, 127, 131

S

Salvador 39, 64, 134, 136, 143, 152, 155, 160, 163-4
samba 41, 43, 45-53, 60-1, 73, 79-81, 84, 121, 133, 136-7, 143-4, 147, 154, 163-4
  rural 52-3
  schools 41, 46, 55-6, 59, 64, 115, 134, 136-7
  term 46
  traditional 52
  variants of 43, 51
samba, carioca 134
samba, songs 54
sambistas 51-2

sanza 59, 86
São Francisco 59, 85
São Paulo 28, 31, 45, 48, 52, 59-60, 64, 141-5, 147, 149-52, 154-7, 159-60, 162-4, 168
 northern coast of 59, 85
sarroncas 92-3
segment 70, 73, 78
semba 41 *see also samba*
Senegal 67
severance, principle of 97-8, 124-5
Shaba 12-13, 16, 22, 72, 84
singers 64, 75, 78, 104, 116
skin pigmentation 25, 61, 89, 91, 136-7
slave markets 20, 26-7, 29
slaveholders 27, 30, 47, 118, 134
social organization 10-11
social sciences 97, 125, 127
societies
 order of 100, 118
 secret 99, 101
songs 39-40, 42, 47-8, 51, 62, 68-9, 74-6, 78, 101-2, 104-5, 107, 109-10, 113, 115, 129
Songye 12
sorghum crop 9-10
souls 11, 106, 112
South Africa 8, 84
Spain 19, 90, 92, 136
stringed instruments 49, 54, 67
structure, social 97-8, 122, 127
style 66, 68, 139, 159
Sudanese 7, 20, 27, 31, 66, 85, 91, 103, 132
syncope 48, 70

T

Tata Mwalaba 107
Teke 6, 11, 20-2
timbre 63

INDEX

time division 56, 76, 80-1, 83, 102, 121, 133
trade 11-12, 18-19, 21-2
trafficking, illegal 133 *see also* enslavement
transatlantic slaving 16, 18-19, 21, 23, 86, 90, 118-20, 124, 135
tuned idiophones 85

U

umbigada 41-3, 46-9, 61, 133, 144, 163
UNESCO 141, 157-8, 161
United States 40, 135-6

V

values (cultural) 10, 15, 37, 91, 100, 103, 111, 113, 115, 118, 120, 125, 128
values, assigned 103, 113, 123, 125, 131
Vansina, Jan 4-5, 12, 15, 157, 160-2
veneration 103, 112
Verger, Pierre 20, 28, 31, 39, 157, 162-3
verses 62, 108, 110
village 72, 91, 108, 114, 116, 125, 128, 130
vocal production 65-6
voice 57, 66, 82, 91, 109, 116-17

W

women 14, 31, 77, 91, 116
  enslaved African 49
wood 50, 59, 61-3, 91, 123

X

xylophones 84, 130

Y

Yaka   4, 6, 14-15, 20-1, 85, 115
Yombe   11

Z

Zaire   4, 68, 75, 110, 116, 149, 153, 168-9
zambombas   92

www.ingramcontent.com/pod-product-compliance
Lightning Source LLC
Chambersburg PA
CBHW051545020426
42333CB00016B/2103